Cycling in Shakespeare Country
And the Vale of the Avon

Ian Watson

cycling
in shakespeare country
and the vale of the avon

ian watson

Once more unto the breach, dear friends, once more;
Or close the wall up with our English dead

Published by
The Perth County Visitor's Association

Also by the author:
Adventure Cycling in the Victorian Kawarthas

Illustrations: Erik Sansom, Stratford, Ontario.
Maps: Ian Watson

Library of Congress Control Number:

ISBN: 1-889602-32-9

10 9 8 7 6 5 4 3 2 1

to tina

My wife and best friend

cycling in shakespeare country and the vale of the avon
ian watson

Contents

Perchance thy taste might be for sausage of the Frankfurt art

stratspeak

Hard by the Queen's Inn, a house of goodly ale and fare, there lies a simple place where bread and meat are had at modest coin. Therein, the elder folk of this blessed town do meet to while away their failing years, to tell their tales of youth and glory in the past and yesteryear.

This simple place, by name the House of Tim, has much to offer in the realm of fare. To eat among the throng or take away to other spots, the House of Tim doth worry not a whit, but wraps such repast in a seemly cloth to spread upon the sward by Avon's stream.

And hark, the stalwart burgers of this town. They come all dressed and with the works of peppers green. With onions fried and love apples sliced upon the slant. All this, and on a loaf so white, as pure as any virgin seen afield. Perchance thy taste might be for sausage of the Frankfurt art, a noble dog unleashed upon the jaws and basted with a sauce of honeyed lard.

On market day, the Merry Wives of Stratford buy fat capons, chines of beef and mutton legs to roast with parsnips sliced in wine. Flagons of mead fermented in crocks of clay, the noble Metheglin of Chaucer's time, do fortify the soul 'gainst winter chills and agues of the blood. Peradventure, on this scene, while Stratford plays its summer acts, bold Falstaff strides his way from inn to inn, and seen in various guise, to tipple taste and testify the value of these bills of fare in quoths, quiffs and quaffs.

Methinks the wines of Stratford, vintnered at the Queen's Quay, the single house of excise in the Town do rival any house of same repute across the land. This house of wines, placed with gentle hand close by the marketplace and in the shadow of the council hall, doth welcome those who travel to our town to slake their thirst and ease their throats among our merry folk. And those who drink the ale of Falstaff's brew, might try their skills at measures varied, the stoup or firkins in a leathern cup, drawn from the wood of English oaks. But those who drink of Hollands may take their measure by the gill or quarten from the stone and served in pewter cups. Around and about this town are many taverns wherein the serf and thane do drink their ales and tell their tales of royal indiscretions, aldermanic peccadillos and games of sporting chance.

Now, hark you as the Cryer shouts. The play is in the offing, the hour draws nigh. He comes with playbills on a pole, while Jack-in-the Green doth sport with wenches fair. What-ho, Lord Leicester's Men play 'The Castle of Perseverance' at the Swan, across the stream by Watergate, a moral, holy play if any one was writ.

An may you, with laughs upon your worthy lips, try the Swan, where the Lord My Admiral's Men do play 'Ralph Roister Doister', a farce of brokered wedlock, whereat the clown, one Mathew Merrygreeke, doth scheme to make a marriage 'twixt Ralph Roister Doister and Madge Mumblecrust, a fishwife, virgin still at sixty-three.

For these and other plays of worthy cause, the price is fair. A single groat, no more the players ask of those who groundlings are. But if thou hast no coin, no groat to spare the play, then bless you. Come by the Cripplegate, where Morris dancers jig, where Mummers act and ballads sing. Happenstance the Troubadours may lute your sweetheart's strings and Jugglers ply their ancient art. Come by the Whittawer's Hall where journeymen of that craft do perform 'Alexander and Campaspe', by Thomas Lyly writ.

And at Aldgate, the gate through Roman Wall, 'The Rose', a smaller house, where plays the tragedy of Montagu and Capulet. See then the foil and epee of that time, the duel and joust, the parries - carte and sixte, the feint and thrust of feud and blood, and weep to see the deaths of rival kin, locked in star-crossed love beyond despair.

See, the banners rise upon each tower. The Plays will shortly strut their hours upon each stage. Hark to the sound of trumpets, the First Sounding, hurry ye. Make haste to what you will, and with the groundlings wait. The Third Sounding blows. The play will now begin.

tour segments

Tour	Km.	Mi.	Page
Mitchell via the Avon Vale	55	34	13
Stratford-St. Marys-Avonton	65	40	23
Stratford-Bimini-Avonton	40	25	30
Stratford-Wartburg-Shakespeare	55	34	45
Stratford-Tavistock-Bimini	45	28	57
Stratford-Monkton-Rostock	75	46	67
Listowel-Milverton	55	34	77
Stratford-Wellesley-Crosshill	85	53	87
St. Marys to Motherwell	30	19	95
Millbank-Brussels-Milverton	100	62	103
Drayton Festival	75	47	111
Little Germany	65	40	119
Woodstock via Hickson	90	56	129
The North Perth Trailway	40	25	135
Wildwood Lake and Harrington	50	31	141
Total Distance for all Tours	925	575	

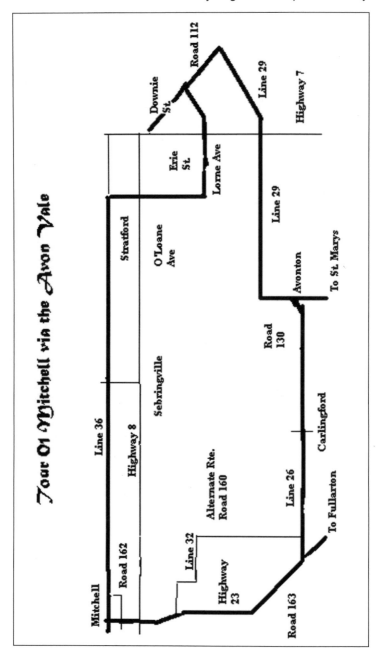

Tour 01 Mitchell via the Avon Vale

mitchell via the avon vale

Distance: 55 kms.
Difficulty: novice to intermediate.
Terrain: mostly flat, with some small hills.
Surface: 99% tarmac, 1% gravel.

"What do you mean by the Veil of the Avon," the Know-It-All asked me, as we pedaled our way out of Stratford. "Shakespeare made a few veiled references in his time, but I didn't know you were capable of such perfidy."

I don't know why I ride with this aggravating creature, but he is an old comrade, and I suppose some day I'll have to fire a volley over his grave, preferably a half volley capable of carrying him well into the hereafter.

"I'm talking about the Vale, not a veil, the poetic term for a valley, where the streams and creeks and ditches and witches and tribulets and capulets all drain into the River Avon!"

I ground my dentures at him for emphasis. My health had suffered somewhat since the Last Supper of roast pork, complete with crackling. It's the crackling, you know, that causes me heartburn from stern to sternum. My wife believes that the way to a man's heart is directly through his rib cage, and when you think of it, she's right.

I was attempting to formalize a route out of Stratford which the whole Pacemakers Club had ridden since Starley first invented the safety bicycle. Back in 1899-1901, there were regular time trial races out of Stratford. Bill, Tom and Fred McCarthy plus Fred and Bill Dunbar were the best known racers of the day. Bill McCarthy's record for the fastest 20 miles ridden out of Stratford, to St. Marys and return, was 56 minutes and 32 seconds. By any standard that ain't hanging about. Hence my interest in creating some routes out of Stratford and keeping these early heroes in mind.

"Don't forget J.A. McFadyen who dominated the Century races at that time," the Know-It-All said, smirking over his superior knowledge of bicycle history. He was right, I'm sorry to say. McFadyen was a pioneer in Century racing.

When you consider the road surfaces of those times, gravel with the crushed bones of early settlers in an amalgam of mud, and bicycles weighing up to 60 pounds, with frames made from gas tubing, their achievements of both speed and endurance are nothing short of miraculous.

Century races 100 years ago were held under the jurisdiction of the Canada Road Club and the 100 miles had to be completed between sunrise and sunset, not an unreasonable rule. These races were held on the highway between Stratford and Goderich, return. Each cyclist carried a card, which had to be signed by the postmaster in three locations along the route, certifying he had ridden through there.

When a rider completed his first Century he was awarded a Silver Century Bar. This has nothing to do with my personal beer recovery rate, which, for a century ride is set very prudently at ten bottles of ale or lager, purely for its anaesthetic value. After ten centuries a rider was awarded a Gold Century Bar, or a free burial, whichever he preferred. Personal choice was a freedom much valued by our Victorian ancestors!

I explained this trivia to the Know-It-All, but he just grunted. I think he was having trouble with his dentures that morning because I'd given him a large slab of toffee and it had locked his top and bottom set together, which stopped much of his yap, a humane course of action. There's always more than one way of getting lockjaw.

With peace and quiet assured, we rode south on Downie Street, crossing Lorne Avenue and continuing south where the route becomes Road 112. At Line 29 we turned west and eventually crossed Highway 7/19, which comes blasting up from St. Marys complete with monster trucks and death wish-drivers.

By this time the Know-It-All was slowly coming out of lockjaw mode and I frantically searched my bike bag for another lump of toffee. Silence continued apart from some noisy birds that insisted on bursting forth into song, heralding a false spring. The weather was unseasonably warm and the last of the snow had gone from the roads, although many pockets still melted where drifts had blown into sheltered banks.

After crossing Highway 7/19 we rode three concessions as far as Road 130 and turned south to Avonton. This village, as its name implies, is right on the Avon River. In the past it had stores and more people than now, but its quiet charm is owed to the Avon as it runs under the road bridge and for a while follows Line 26 west, but then turns south through Avonbank and its eventual meeting with the Thames River,

"Do you have any more of that toffee?" the Know-It-All asked, as we pedaled up a slight incline out of Avonton on Line 26. "It has a slight flavor of molasses and diesel fuel," he said, endorsing the toffee's bona fides. I remember buying two pounds of the stuff at a Holy Catholic Church bazaar and that several dogs in the street had turned it down in favor of some cherry nougat produced by the Legion Ladies Auxiliary. Dogs do not suffer from lockjaw of the dentures.

For some time we had climbed up the next stream valley, the

Know-It-All suffering a bit because he found it hard to breathe through his ears, his nose and throat obstructed as they were by the Holy Catholic toffee.

So, when we freewheeled down to Carling Creek and rested at the bridge, he finally got his dentures freed up using one of his tire levers. He then washed both dental plates in the creek, which probably did them no end of good, but frightened the smaller fish. The road continued through Carlingford so we felt compelled to follow. Carlingford is almost a ghost town, the former garage and forge are boarded up. The old school house is now a home and the community center is an old building dating from Victorian times. Just about a kilometer further on is Carlingford Cemetery, a splendid place for anyone trying to trace his or her ancestors. Not a few of the headstones are cut from limestone, a soft material that weathers rapidly. This type of gravestone was commonly used because the material was locally quarried and could be worked by local craftsmen. Later, with the coming of the canals and railways, stonemasons from Scotland and England came out looking for work and the era of granite memorials was born.

We pushed on to Perth Road 163, which headed northwest to Highway 23. It was only a short ride into Mitchell, but a distance where extreme caution has to be exercised. We kept to the edge of the road and when large trucks came by we actually rode on the gravel shoulder. For those who would rather avoid the main road, you can always take Road 160 instead of Road 163 and Highway 23. But it's gravel and some people don't like to grovel in gravel. Road 160 goes north to Line 32 where you can bear west and come awful close to Mitchell. But you're a wimp if you do!

In Mitchell we ate our sandwich lunch in the Lions Park, the Know-It-All being too cheap to spring for bangers and mash in the local Gag and Vomit. We saw no lions in the park, which I thought rather disappointing. I had visions of throwing the Know-It-All to the lions, toffee and all. Score one for the Christians. After lunch and a snooze in the late winter sun, we pushed our bikes across the dam and rode north up the riverside trail as far as Francis Street. Well, you can't go any further, so we rode east on Francis, crossed Highway 23, the Listowel Road, and rode to Road 162, a gravel stretch going north to Line 36. This is the 0.9% gravel that I promised you! So, enjoy.

With the toffee out of his dentures, the Know-It-All grew talkative, but I managed to tune him out. We rode steadily with a following wind to Road 135, the Sebringville road. Our water bottles were empty by this time and I felt a certain level of dementia creep over me. This had its benefits because it made his prattle marginally acceptable. Pushing on, and with a freshening wind elevating our kilts, we soon reached Stratford at O'Loane Avenue, where the Know-It-All said he wanted to be O'Loane and after reaching my house I obliged him by slamming the door and drinking my own beer.

I did say that this ride is 99% tarmac surface with 1% gravel - that's Road 162 that I mentioned previously. Of course you can also miss out the riverside trail and ride on Highway 23 north through Mitchell up to Line 36, but if you do then you're a wimp and I'll never speak to you again. If you feel inclined, that is if you have a talent for leaning either to port or starboard, you can take the gravel road detour one concession west of Avonton and go north to visit all your relatives in Sebringville. I suppose it would be the chummy thing to do if you feel like it, only don't expect them to turn out the village band just because you decided to turn up uninvited.

You might also detour north up Road 135 to Wartburg, but I can't think why unless you suffer from warts, in which case you have my deepest and heartfelt sympathy.

Splat! Right onto his Abercrombie and Fitch bush shirt

"as the worm turns"

You know those 'good news, bad news' jokes? Well, first the bad news.

SOMEBODY in the Pacemakers Cycling Club invited the club Know-It-All to our private fishing trip. This trip has happened for years and we generally pick a back lake where perch and pickerel jump onto the hooks to commit suicide; where there are fish so wild they leap straight into the skillet, ready for a shore lunch. Bullroar.

These lakes are subject to the Official Secrets Act. Nobody gets to go there unless he's checked out for loyalty to Canada, the Crown, the Loony, or anything else potty you can think of.

Knowing all this and knowing the awful penalties for betraying the 'Secrets of the Back Lakes', SOMEBODY still invited the Know-It-All. You will appreciate what a serious breach of security this is when I tell you the penalties. Banishment to Hamilton, Ontario. Thirty days listening to Senator Jesse Helms without his dentures talking about Gum Control and Blaming It On Canada. Burrs and hitch hikers sewn inside your Spandex under garments for a period not exceeding six months.

For the purpose of this story you have to understand that a select few from the Pacemakers go bicycle fishing. This is not a process whereby the angler dunks a hook into some unsuspecting pond or creek and comes up with a bike on the end of his line.

No. Bicycle fishing is an extreme sport of its own and consists of taking light spinning tackle with a pack rod, and loading the whole kit into bike bags, then fishing in the more remote places where four-by-fours, all terrain vehicles and armored personnel carriers cannot follow.

Bicycle fishing is, therefore, an extreme sport in every sense of the word and not meant for the faint of heart. It may be fine for the weak of mind or for those bordering on an interesting mental breakdown, but it's not for the faint of heart.

During the evenings planning the trip, telling stretchers - 'do you remember when' - sort of stretchers, the usual, time honored process was ruined by the Know-It-All's monopoly of the stories. He'd shot lions in Africa, tigers in India, crocodiles up the Nile. To be shot up the Nile sounded quite painful and we told him so, but he corrected us in his patient way.

"You have to shoot crocodiles right between the eyes, other-wise the bullet just bounces off because their skulls are so numb." We'd always wondered what a numbskull was. Now we knew. What a croc.

When the day of the fishing trip dawned, the Pacemakers

Bike Anglers picked up the Great White Know-It-All. There was an awesome hush as he wheeled his bicycle down the garden path to join us. Who were we to question the skill of a man who had shot things all over the world? So nobody had the gall to blindfold him when we got close to our special lake.

We rode to the north shore where some overhangs masked a deep hole. This was where the lunkers lurked. The Know-It-All looked pasty, white around the gills. I thought it was some sort of motion sickness caused by the badly rutted trail we had ridden. Nelson, Hornblower, Farragut, heroes all, suffered from seasickness. Maybe there was a rutted trail sickness!

We had plenty of bait; fat red and black worms dug from the compost heaps. We baited our hooks, cast and waited. All except the Know-It-All.

"Would you put a worm on my hook, dear fellow," he said, his stomach
heaving.

A sense of evil warmed my black heart. Slowly I selected a fine juicy specimen from the bait box. Surgically I threaded the fattest of worms onto his hook, stretching the operation out so he could see all the gory details in glorious color. I swung the rig towards him. Splat! Right onto his Abercrombie and Fitch bush shirt.

The noise of him retching uncontrollably into the weeds behind us was deeply satisfying and music to our ears. He didn't speak for the rest of the trip.

That's the good news.

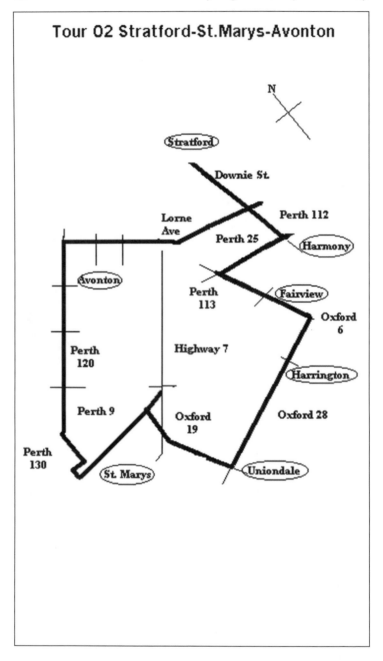

stratford - st. marys - avonton

Distance: 65 kms.
Difficulty: intermediate.
Terrain: rolling to hilly, with many flat stretches.
Surface: 100% tarmac.

"The last time I rode this little tour, I had some visitors with me," I told the Know-It-All as we waited at the corner of Downie Street and Lorne Avenue on Stratford's south side. "The visitors had an original bicycling map of Perth County and they fancied this route, and they only asked me to go along with them because they were concerned about hills. 'Were there any hills?' I told them that hills around here were 'Much Ado About Nothing' and let 'em stew in that one all morning."

The Know-It-All just grunted. He was still picking bacon and sausage from his dentures because Mrs. Know-It-All was away and he'd treated himself to breakfast at the Comedy of Errors coffee shop. Finally, he walked over to a fire hydrant where the Works people were flushing the water mains. He rinsed his dentures in the runoff and I think they felt more comfortable afterwards.

It was two minutes to nine in the forenoon watch. Bugle Brain and Foghorn, the Club Hammerheads, joined us. I told them both politely to shut up. There's nothing like establishing your authority, but they just ignored me and blew raspberries, startling an old lady walking her dog.

We shoved off south of Lorne Avenue. Downie Street turns itself into Perth Road 112 so we resolved to humor it and go along with the idea. Roads have wills of their own and since all this 'trickle down' sharing of the tax wealth and local empowerment, country roads have become unbearable and full of their own self-importance.

"This used to be County Road 21," Bugle Brain complained. "My map says County Road 21 and now they've put up signage saying it's Perth Road 112."

"Quit your moaning and buy a new map," Foghorn advised, rather pragmatically, I thought.

The uninformed would imagine that Perth County has put bike lanes on this road. There's a two-foot path with a white line, just itching to be called a bike lane. But knowing local authorities, I know the two-foot path is there for a more subtle reason. I think they use this road, and a few others like it, to train people in the art of drawing white lines with one of those machines. In winter, they train Zamboni drivers on stretches of the 401. I have the skid marks to prove it.

After a steady ride we arrived at the small village of Harmony. When our kids were little we used to picnic at the park, but now the road is no longer quiet since they surfaced it, using it to link Highways 59 and 7.

Nostalgia aside, we turned right onto Perth Road 26. The Avon Trail passes just to the north of Harmony and the trail markers are white blazes. Do not, under any circumstances, take your bicycle onto this trail. The Avon Trail is a hiking trail only and I would personally shoot any death-wish mountain biker I saw using it. And I am a dead shot with a peashooter. If you ride a bike, ride it on the road and don't mess with other good people's pastime.

The bike lane continues as you ride west (or east if you feel like it) and we got into single file, burning the rubber as far as the yellow flashing light at Perth Road 113. The country starts to become rolling on this stretch and riding single file, occasionally changing the lead rider to keep the pace lively, we turned left onto Perth Road 113 and went south.

This is real rolling stuff and we rolled all the way to Fairview. At this point the road becomes uppity and gives itself another name. It becomes known as Oxford Road 6, which is OK I suppose because we were now in Oxford County. Bugle Brain and Foghorn checked their visas and found they were OK for Oxford, so we rode down the hill, hooting and hollering, and then up the other side, spluttering and spitting.

Arriving at Oxford Road 28, the Know-It-All decided to check the map, probably because he wanted to take a breather. "You guys should take a breather," he told us. The guy's all heart.

After chewing on bonk bars and sucking back on Gatorade (you have to support the sponsors), we turned right onto Oxford Road 28, riding towards the village of Harrington. The country is rolling to hilly, adding to your existing high state of cardio-vascular health. I've never met any Cardiovasculars, but I suppose they are quite nice people, foreign, but otherwise quite nice.

Over the years (thirty to be precise) that I've ridden a bicycle around here, Harrington has closed its stores. So take your own bonk bars and Gatorade.

I remember a community barbecue held at the old school house, back when we had little children. Our daughter was only five then and we still have a Stratford Beacon-Herald picture of her with her teeth firmly locked into a chicken leg. She's a vegetarian now.

There's a small park in Harrington run by the Upper Thames Conservation Authority. It's quiet and there are a few picnic tables and loos of the thunder box genre when in season. What people do when thunder boxes are out of season I have no idea and have a closed mind on the matter. The Know-It-All says that Canadians are trained to observe universal winter abstinence.

For those who like to keep statistics, and I'm not one of them, it is twenty kilometers from Stratford to Harrington on this route. There, I've done my duty.

The bonk bars and Gatorade and all that jazz, must have done us good because we swept up the hill going west out of Harrington looking like a mountain breakaway in the Tour de France. Fortunately, the road flattens at the top of the hill and we rode into Uniondale where we stood around in a variety of poses in case the local people wanted to take photographs of us. Nobody took any notice. I suppose they had never seen people like us before and they thought it best to stay indoors until we had left.

Uniondale is on Oxford Road 119 and I know you were waiting to hear that. We turned right and rode to the crossing at Highway 7. There's a big stop sign there and a restaurant called Woolfey's. We crossed Highway 7 and noticed that Oxford Road 119 is then miraculously transformed into Perth Road 118. We thanked Queen's Park for further trickle down evidence. The Know-It-All said that Queen's Park has trickled down on him for years and Bugle Brain and Foghorn told him to shaddup.

It was not too far to the stop at Perth Road 9. Turning left and heading towards St. Marys, this road renames itself as Queen Street. Roads can be real snobs.

St. Marys is a beautiful place, whether its roads are snobs or not. From the stone water tower we descended the hill in style, prepared to accept the applause which we richly deserved. Strangely, nobody clapped and nobody cheered. Nobody even looked at us. I suppose the St. Maryites are far too pleased with their town to notice four strangers in their midst riding bikes. Rightly so because stone buildings are everywhere. You would need a month in St. Marys to study the architecture and the sheer workmanship of the stone masons.

We rode down the hill to the third stop light and turned right onto Water Street North. It was noon and people's stomachs were chiming twelve. We lunched by the river and then Bugle Brain and Foghorn played Frisbee in the park, catching the Frisbee in their teeth. Those two are a little strange. The sun was warm and I had my back to a stone wall. Pretty soon I dozed off. When I woke, the Know-It-All was still asleep, his head rolling around in circles, missing a pinnacle of rock by a mere sixteenth of an inch. I screwed up my lunch bag and pitched it at him. It took him squarely on the end of his nose, which caused him to roll his head in the opposite direction and bang his head against the stone pinnacle, placed there for that express purpose.

"Who put that infernal.....?" Just then, Bugle Brain and Foghorn returned from playing Frisbee and they got the blame for the pinnacle of rock being where it had been for a hundred years.

From our lunch spot by the bridge on Water Street, we turned right onto Parkway Drive. The Know-It-All was being ornery, but that's nothing new. At the stop on Parkview and Wellington we jogged left and then right onto Station Road. Once more, miracles happened. Station Road became James Street North as it bends near the railway overpass. As it exits St. Marys, the road becomes Perth Road 130.

This all sounds complicated but it's not really. However, I'll bet you get lost. We lost the Know-It-All as we rode up the hill out of St. Marys. I thought this was a blessing in disguise, but Bugle Brain said that the Know-It-All had only gone over to see the old Union Station. We circled back and sure enough we found the Know-It-All again. There's a green fingerboard directing you to the old Union building so I expect the temptation proved too much for him.

We headed towards Avonton. It seemed to be the decent thing to do! Riding pursuit style like something from the Olympic games of 1902, we mopped up the klicks to Avonton, crossing Perth Road 20 on the way.

Avonton was quiet as we passed through. It always is and it's highly possible that the Mayor of Avonton has invoked a curfew. I've never seen anybody there and sometimes I think it was the blueprint for Oliver Goldsmith's 'Deserted Village'.

Not far north of Avonton, after granny gearing it up the hill, we turned onto Line 29 and rode east. Eventually we came to Highway 7 and stopped because we didn't want to be squashed by trucks. We made the Know-It-All ride point, and after crossing Highway 7 we rode like banshees to the stop at Perth Road 113. Crossing this, we rode on like MacDuff and all his cronies to Perth Road 112 where we turned left and north back to Stratford.

The road became Downie Street again, which was to be expected. Bugle Brain and Foghorn rode home making awful honking noises, and I rode with the Know-It-All to his house in the event that he might have a stock of beer, but he went inside and shut the door. He is so mean spirited!

for the fat-tired gravel grovelers

An extra 10 klicks over gravel, for the tough and sinewy is a little diversion off Perth Road 130 as you steam north out of St. Marys. Make a left on Line 14 and ride one concession west to Perth Road 134. Go right and head north. After much hardship you will arrive at Perth Line 32 (Lorne Avenue) where you turn right onto this splendid road and it takes you back to your start point, provided you do the pedaling! Sarcastic old devil!

The spy who was too stupid to come in from the cold

a man called insipid

We were indebted to Jane Eyre-Head for the use of her splendid new van on the day we decided to venture across the County border, drive through the Jungles of Oxford and enter the Region of Haldimand-Norfolk.

Jane was chaperoned that day by Kalashnikov Kate who suffered from a grave loss of voice due to a hereditary allergy. Kate cannot eat peanuts or any form of peanut products. It's easily done. Kate stopped at a bake sale in Harrington village and bought some cookies. You guessed it. The bake cook had used peanut butter, a healthful food in itself, but not if you're allergic to it.

Kate immediately lost her voice and we expected this silent intermission to prevail throughout the week. The Know-It-All asked a rhetorical question about what would happen to a monkey who had a peanut allergy. One would expect his days to be mercifully numbered. The Know-It-All, that is.

We left Stratford very early, while the morning star was still burning bright. It's a long drive to the City of Simcoe where we intended to pick up the Llyn Valley Trail and ride south as far as Port Dover. In Dover we had a rendezvous with a lunch menu of fish and chips before riding across country to Vittoria and then returning to Simcoe and Jane Eyre-Head's van.

That was the game plan, and all went well until we got to Port Dover and the Know-It-All suddenly burst forth with one of his pronouncements. "There's a proverb," he said. "Spies are the ears and eyes of princes."

I wondered why he said that, but strongly suspected I would regret something badly that day if I questioned him. He was due to give one of his frequent historical ear-bashes and we had just read a historical plaque about the burning of Port Dover.

"Spies were everywhere during the War of 1812," he said, warming to his subject. He seated himself on a bench at the waterfront, gathering an audience of visitors and seagulls who just happened to be near. I knew the inevitable was about to occur and cursed myself roundly because I had forgotten to pack my earplugs along with my pills and Gatorade.

"Some of our ancestors (here he gestured towards me and I knew I was irretrievably drawn into this ear-bash session), were involved. At that time, both our families had serving members of the 69th Infantry Regiment, the Duke of Athlete's Foot. The Old Sixty-Ninth was part of the Imperial Force of regulars, garrisoned at Vittoria to stiffen the Militia ranks."

So far, this was somewhat true. Both our families had served in the Duke of Athlete's Foot since it was raised quite recently in 1688. During the years following, the Sixty-Ninth had fought in a couple of minor engagements like the American Rebellion in 1776 and the War of 1812 (which went on until 1815). We were with Wellington at Waterloo, the Zulu War, both World Wars, Korea, and also participated in the Arabian Field Force of 1949-1951. It was during this last engagement that I shared a tent with the Know-It-All and six other squaddies of the Sixty-Ninth. He was comparatively mild back then: a bit snobby, claiming that he was educated at Duke of Wellington College, but I learned that he'd been booted out! I remember he was a rotten soldier. He was such a coward he had a local anesthetic before he cut his toenails.

He continued. "In fact, if it hadn't been for a squad of troopers from the Duke of Athlete's Foot, the Burning of Port Dover would have spread right along the Lakeshore, from Fort Erie all the way to Windsor. This tiny group foiled the 800 or so American troops, under the command of Lieutenant-Colonel John Campbell, in their attempt.

"The American military force had an agent acting for them on Canadian soil. He is variously identified as a chandler's clerk, Erasmus Helms, or the second mate of the schooner 'City of Dresden', Hiram Carlow. A third possibility is one of the Fenians, whose name was never revealed. Perhaps all three were traitors.

"Throughout the winter of 1813-14, this covert agent worked to uncover the plans for the building of a naval dockyard at Port Dover. This work was the original inspiration of John Graves Simcoe, the first governor of Upper Canada. After Governor Simcoe left Upper Canada in 1794, no further work was done on the naval dockyard until the War of 1812 broke out. It was only towards the latter part of the war that the need for a dockyard became apparent." By this time the pigeons were becoming restless and the tourists were jumping up and down on their perches. Some pigeons sat on the stools provided. These were called stool pigeons! Totally ignoring how much he bored his audience, the Know-It-All continued his little dockside chat.

"One cannot say that this spy, whatever his real name was, should be regarded as the least bit intelligent, although his profession was supposed to be that of intelligence. In fact he was so ineffectual, so weak and namby-pamby, that he was code-named 'Inspid', or 'A Man Called Inspid'. His lack of effectiveness in the espionage circles of 1812-1815, also caused him to be dubbed 'The Spy Who Was Too Stupid To Come In From The Cold'

"There is some evidence, although evidence from family sources, therefore classified as hearsay in official circles, but probably fact in the history of the Duke of Athlete's Foot, that Inspid had been 'turned' by the squaddies who were serving on detachment from the Regiment to stiffen the local Militia.

"This detachment squad consisted of ancestors of myself, the Little Fat Guy, Buffalo Bilge, Junkyard George, Wild Bill Hiccup, Filthy Rich and Bugle Brain. The last of this squad named for posterity was our trumpeter.

"One never knows how a secret agent is turned. The squad of seven, plus Alf Newport its sergeant - who does not have a nom-de-guerre because he was a 25 year man - were experts in the distillation of Old Embalming Fluid, a spirit of surprisingly smooth quality. This spirit was guaranteed to put hairs on the chest of Lady Simcoe herself, when in season. When Lady Simcoe was in season, that is. This noble distillation must not be confused with inferior brands such as 'Skullbuster' or 'Elephant's Breath'. No, sir. Any brand of firewater smooth enough to put hairs on Lady Simcoe's chest was good enough to persuade a traitor to be turned back to the Canadian cause.

"And that's what happened. The Detachment Squad from A. Company of the Duke of Athlete's Foot, under the command of Sergeant Alf Newport, got the Man Called Insipid crocked out of his skull. He was then placed in a compromising position with two naked Port Dover maidens and, since this all happened before photography was invented, a local painter of watercolors, William Pope, painted the scarlet scene. Although usually recognized as a wildlife artist, Pope's rendering of the wild life featuring Insipid and the Port Dover nudes was sufficient to blackmail the spy into supplying false and misleading information to the American assault force under Lieutenant-Colonel Campbell.

"This false information took the form of inflating the eight squad members into a regiment sized force of over 800. Laying false trails, marching and counter marching, the Old Sixty-Ninth men led the Campbell Force round and round in so many circles that they thought they were part of a second Revolution. After all, a revolution is but one turn in an ever-decreasing circle.

"Although there was much damage, it could have been far worse had it not been for the cunning of the Old Sixty-Ninth and Alf Newport's squad in particular. Finally, the Americans were so disoriented and so dispirited due to their failure in bringing this phantom force to battle, that they gave up and went home to their mothers who were temporarily quartered at Fort Erie."

The pigeons clapped their wings by way of applause, which pleased the Know-It-All no end. The visitors had all fallen asleep and became grumpy when he tried to take up a collection by passing his hat around. The results were not all that encouraging: seven cents in pennies - all Canadian, a gum wrapper, two Chicago

Subway tokens, a handful of twist tops and an invitation to Gospel Hour - 'All Welcome'.

The Know-It-All cleared his throat and went on. "According to the Regimental history of the Duke of Athlete's Foot, the identity of the squad who performed this masterpiece of counter-espionage and psychological warfare, is correctly recorded. The identity of Insipid is still secret and has never been revealed under the Freedom of Information Act because it would become too sensitive an issue. It is strongly believed, however, by veterans of the Sixty-Ninth, that ancestors of Kalashnikov Kate and Jane Eyre-Head were the two naked Port Dover maidens involved in the compromising plot and subsequent watercolor. My lips are sealed; I am gagged by circumstances.

"On a more positive note I have to record that the Americans burned Port Dover on May 16, 1814. In retaliation for this act, the Duke of Athlete's Foot marched as a flying column to Washington and burned the White House to the ground on August 24th in the same year, using Old Embalming Fluid as an incendiary. This final act of war forced the belligerents into a cessation of hostilities, subsequently formalized at the Treaty of Ghent.

"This totally ticked off President James Madison because there had been no water in the White House to put out the fire when the Old Sixty-Ninth paid their visit in 1814. So, when the Executive Mansion was rebuilt in 1817, priority was given for piped firewater! This was finally provided, and as part of the peace treaty, a permanent contract for supplying Old Embalming Fluid to the President of the United States fell to the Original Eight and has been passed down to their descendents since 1833.

"As for Alf Newport. He was promoted to Regimental Sergeant Major, turned into a brass mold back at the Regimental Depot and has been used to shape RSMs ever since."

It was the middle of the afternoon before this historical diatribe was finished. The tourists vanished and the seagulls went back to work. Naturally, Kalashnikov Kate had been silent throughout the Know-It-All's speech, due to her loss of voice. Her spirit was still there, and like all revolutionaries she believed in action not words. In one swift, fluid motion Kate gripped the Know-It-All warmly and firmly by the throat, shaking him as a terrier does a rat. Terror shot from his eyes and he fell to the jetty clutching at his epiglottis.

But it did the trick. He was silent, apart from the occasional gurgle, all the way back to Simcoe. Driving back to Stratford in Jane's van was also fairly tranquil except when we got near the first Tim's on the East Side. "Coffee," he croaked. Such an appeal can never be refused, even from the Know-It-All.

Wonder of wonders. The Know-It-All put his hand into his pocket and treated everyone!

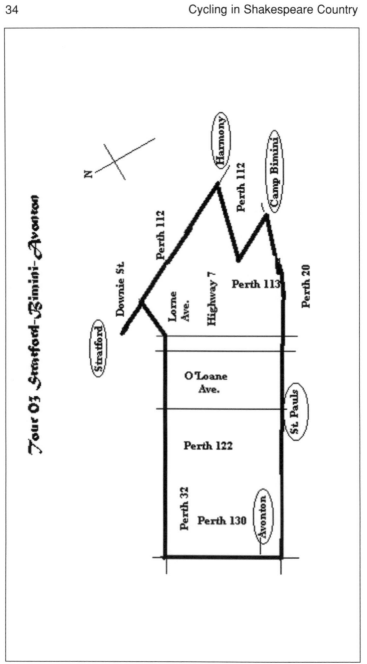

stratford - Bimini - avonton

Distance: 40 kms.
Difficulty: novice to intermediate.
Terrain: flat to rolling.
Surface: 100% tarmac.

This little route is good for a lone ride, one of those rides when you want to disappear for a few hours to think and then come back home in a sadder and wiser mood.

As I live on the south side of Stratford, some would say on the wrong side of the tracks, my usual starting point for this route is the junction of Downie Street and Lorne Avenue. It also happens to be the site of the Customer Delight Restaurant where bacon, sausages, eggs and other succulents are dealt off the arm, provided that your pension's just come in and you have enough moolah to cover the bill.

Riding south on Perth Road 112, which is only Downie Street by another name, I perceived that this road encourages a rider to work up a steady pace and I needed to shake winter out of my joints. I'd just had a knee examination by some orthopedic chap, Saul of Metatarsis I think he was called, who pronounced joyfully that I had arthritis and he couldn't do anything about it short of amputation. What a delightful thought. Happily, the knee didn't hurt when I rode my bike, only when I had to scrub the floors during spring cleaning and I thought I'd contracted housemaid's knee. This is the sort of introspection one can endure on a lone ride.

The winding up and the steady pace soon brought me to the Great Flashing Light at Harmony. Traffic was sparse that day except for a large livestock truck full of pigs and I have never been able to look a pork chop in the eye after that.

Fortunately I was riding in the opposite direction to the pigs, having made a right in Harmony and riding west on Perth Road 26. Flashing lights are very popular and after one up-and-down hill I came to the yellow flashing light at Perth Road 113. The route goes left and south here, so I did the same. Just a couple of kilometers along this road, down a nice hill, which has its own stream at the bottom, you turn right onto Line 20.

This is Camp Bimini. There's nothing clandestine about it; it's not like Camp X in Oshawa where they trained hundreds of secret agents in World War II. Camp Bimini is very quiet and even the trout in the stream are the silent type.

Anyway, Line 20 keeps up the local tradition for hills and I granny geared up a slight rise because I felt decidedly delicate that morning. It was probably due to looking at all those pork chops on the hoof or trotter or whatever pork chops run on. It's a nice tree-lined road through farmland until you get to the Highway, which used to be called Highway 7, but has now been changed to Perth Road 119, and has probably developed a complex about it.

Of course you stop here because it's dangerous. There is evidence of groundhogs who failed to stop and paid the ultimate penalty. I stopped because of the traffic light, but soon crossed and continued on Line 20 to the village of St. Paul's. There's a splendid ballpark, picnic shelter and washrooms when in season. The little store and post office is now closed. I suppose that's called progress.

The South Perth office is at this crossroad. I don't know if that helps. You might feel better about government in general if you knew that, but then you might not.

I turned right, onto Perth Road 122 going north and crossed the tracks, riding up to the next stop at Line 26 where I hung a left. This route takes you through flattish farmland with tree-lined roads. It's the type of farmland that I would describe as prosperous, but I know I'm wrong because all the farmers I talk to tell me that they lose money and that soon there will be no food left in the world. It's an endless source of worry for me. I am also left with the impression that any farmer who makes money has the wrong accountant.

I shrugged off my agricultural depression and rode west to Avonton. I suppose you could stop in Avonton, maybe stare at the River Avon and wonder how Shakespeare thought up all those characters like Iago, particularly Iago, who is so much like the Know-It-All.

Anyone who has tread left on his tires and who wants a little gravel included in the ride, should take a small detour south from Avonton on Perth Road 130 as far as Line 16 and then hang a right. This takes you (on a road surface with stones and tar, rather like nutty chocolate) into Avonbank, a small hamlet on the Avon River. (The entire world knows that a hamlet is a child actor!) Continue west to Perth Road 134; turn right at the Presbyterian Church and head north on gravel. Cross Line 20 and at Line 26 go right again on tarmac and back to Avonton, where you will find those with more sense than you still staring into the Avon River.

The reason why they are all staring into the Avon is traditional. I was responsible, about 100 years ago, for naming this little gravelly bit as "The Road To Avonbank", a groaner of the Nth degree, more so when the C.B.C. heard about it! This splendid look at rural Avon country is 13 klicks, although the Know-It-All claims it to be only ten klicks with a following zephyr up your kilt and over 15 with a head wind. Go figure. Those who took this diversion will then celebrate what splendid fellows they are and sneer at the others for the rest of the day.

Well, now everybody's back together, unless you're riding by yourself, head north up Perth Road 130 to Line 32. Turn right and ride east until you reach the intersection at O'Loane Avenue, the Stratford boundary. Keep going east on Lorne Avenue, up the hill to the lights at Erie Street. Cross and continue on Lorne Avenue back to your start point at Downie Street.

This is a favorite route for me if I want a short jaunt in the morning or afternoon. I generally use my road bike for impressing the young girls. In winter I use my touring bike with fenders and Goretex stuff. I never take a lunch. Well, maybe a bonk bar and always a water bottle. I always ride this route clockwise. One day I will learn to live dangerously and ride it counterclockwise.

She seems to have an early warning system

the monday to friday dog

We were riding out near Carlingford one sunny autumn morning, just myself and the club Know-It-All, when he started in on something quite fresh. It was not that I was particularly interested in his thesis, because my mind was elsewhere and this forced me to grunt every twenty seconds to show some level of understanding with what he was jawing about.

My mind was on the set of clipless pedals I had just put on my road bike and in a practical sense getting used to the cleats. I had fallen off at a traffic light in Stratford by not uncleating fast enough and a school crossing guard picked me up before the little children in her care could poke me with sticks.

"I firmly believe that the Bard of Avon must have been bilingual and beat official bilingualism by about four hundred years," the Know-It-All droned, as we changed gears for the long grind up the hill at Carlingford Cemetery. "Look how he wrote those lines for the princess in Henry V." I grunted, hopefully it was a bilingual grunt, suitable for a French princess.

We rode on and I was becoming a little bit anxious about the clipless pedals because we were in range of Dead Pig Farm where the Monday to Friday Dog lives. You have to be a bit nifty when you pass Dead Pig Farm because the Monday to Friday Dog, while only a Jack Russell Terrier, is on steroids and quite capable of jumping a five-bar gate from a standing start. I suppose this dog is really a Jane Russell Terrier, being a female of the species. That is quite unimportant at this time.

"I have a feeling that Shakespeare's original name was Shakes-Pierre. That's how he knew enough French to write the princess's lines in Hank Five-O." This is an example of just how silly the Know-It-All is getting in his old age. He's so daft that he won't try clipless pedals and says he'd rather ride with pedal-less clips.

The Monday to Friday Dog has been the bane of the Pacemakers Cycling Club for three seasons. She hates cyclists and the more cyclists who pass her farm gate the better she likes it because then she can hate all the more cyclists. This dog has been responsible for more downfalls, literally, of cyclists as they pass Dead Pig Farm, than you can shake a stick at, or perhaps a dog leash.

She seems to have an early warning system, a type of radar, which detects approaching cyclists from at least one concession's distance. With this warning she's off the runway and gaining altitude, ready to attack out of the sun. In summary, she's a darned nuisance. Her yap is worse than the Know-It-All's because it's in dog language, a language about one notch higher than the Know-It-All's.

The Monday to Friday Dog's Finest Hour came with the downing of five club members in one attack. I am embarrassed to state that it was a dogfight. I was the first club member to bite the dust that day while the Monday to Friday Dog scurried around on the township road outside Dead Pig Farm, ripping and snapping at bare ankles and the more ample flesh of cyclists further up the leg.

Kalashnikov Kate crashed next, cursing and swearing about all capitalists. I had no idea that the Monday to Friday Dog was a capitalist dog. I suppose anything's possible if a dog owns a farm like Dead Pig Farm. Kate was shortly joined by Buffalo Bilge who had swerved to avoid Jane Eyre-Head and ran full tilt into Wild Bill Hiccup. Wild Bill went over the top of the handlebars and slid into a morass of pig effluent. It was Wild Bill's helmet that saved his life that day because he hit the pig effluent headfirst.

There was a lull in the proceedings while we were joined by James Bondage, a recent recruit to the Pacemakers and who had stopped back at the last concession road to attend to a call of nature. During this lull, a time period common to all the better dogfights, the Monday to Friday Dog had shot back to the farmhouse where a human hand had emerged from the kitchen door and thrown a large bone at her. I can only believe that the bone came from a freshly dead cyclist.

With the bone firmly in her jaws, this diminutive pooch, the Monday to Friday Dog, rejoined the fray at exactly the same time as James Bondage appeared on the scene. Like a streak of canine lightning, the Monday to Friday Dog attacked James Bondage on his starboard beam. As fast as greased lightning she shot under our new member's bottom bracket and chainwheel without pausing and with the human bone still in her teeth.

James Bondage had no time to bail out or free his feet from the pedal cleats. He piled on top of Buffalo Bilge and Wild Bill. Everyone swore and cursed according to his or her political lights, the worst invective coming from Kalashnikov Kate. I was past swearing because sudden contact with the county road had driven every ounce of breath from my lungs. Buffalo Bilge and Wild Bill both cursed in true western fashion, condemning all eastern sodbusters to early and uncomfortable graves.

The Monday to Friday Dog sat there by the mailbox, occasionally scratching her back on the post. She dropped the bone, daring anyone from the Pacemakers to touch it.

James Bondage was the last to pick himself up. I thought he would order himself a vodka martini on the rocks, stirred, not shaken, but he just said, "Oh, bother," as he surveyed the wreckage.

The Monday to Friday Dog, undaunted by odds, unwearied by constant challenge and mortal danger, sat there panting. Never in the field of dog versus human conflict was so much owed to clipless pedals.

Every dog has her day and the Monday to Friday Dog knew her limit. She was an ace. She knew that, having just scored her fifth 'destroyed' plus two 'probables' and two 'seriously damaged' that she had reached the heights of Billy Bishop and Chuck Yeager. She looked at us, grinning as only a Jane Russell Terrier can.

We mounted up and rode away from this scene of carnage because the Know-It-All and Jane Eyre-Head were oblivious to the effects of the attack, riding on and leaving us to the full extent of the ambush.

The reader may wonder at the choice of the name I have given to this hound, the Monday to Friday Dog. Bitter experience has shown us that she only mounts these attacks against cyclists from Monday to Friday. She works a strict 8:00 a.m. to 4:30 p.m., five-day work week with a half hour lunch and two fifteen minute paid bone breaks. A regular supply of fresh human bones is part of her contract in the pay and fringe benefits clause.

The Monday to Friday Dog has complete charge of Dead Pig Farm during these times. She never attacks on Saturdays and Sundays because the human adults, the mortgage holders of the farm, and the children, those who fill her up with chocolate and bubble gum and make her sick, are home. Peanut butter wouldn't melt in her mouth on Saturdays and Sundays.

Mondays are the worst time to run foul of this animal. On Mondays she suffers badly from a chocolate and bubble gum hangover, when the children are at school. She's testy, snarly and bad tempered, and her head and stomach just kill her. Even if you try and sneak past Dead Pig Farm when she's trying to sleep off the hangover, her radar system gives early warning and she scrambles before you're anywhere close.

But on the day of this diabolical attack she must have felt generous, a kind of TGIF generosity, because it was late Friday and I suppose she was getting ready to punch out. We got away and eventually caught the Know-It-All and Jane Eyre-Head out near Fullarton, by the Black Creek Bridge on line 29.

It was a good thing we caught up with them there because they would have continued west and gone to Winnipeg instead of turning south through Fullarton Village. This would have happened because the Know-It-All was still talking and therefore not paying attention to the route, and Jane Eyre-Head is as dense as a London fog - which is so dense as to be as thick as yellow pea soup.

All this flashed through my mind as I rode with the Know-It-All towards Dead Pig Farm, and while I worried myself stiff about the clipless pedals I had just installed on my road bike. Given that it was a Saturday and therefore the Monday to Friday Dog was off watch. I suppose she thought of herself as a watchdog and Saturday was the dogwatch. Whatever.

The Know-It-All was still cracking on about Shakespeare, or Shakes-Pierre as he now termed the bard, and the bilingual bits of 'Hank Five-O'. He was convinced that the great battle scene had been set by Shakes-Pierre in a suburb of Toronto - at Agincourt, to be precise. But I was too mentally exhausted to argue with him.

As we swept along the road by the row of elm trees, which forms the approach to Dead Pig Farm, we spied a gathering of cyclists at the farm gate. For one awful moment I thought there had been a massacre, a sort of ethnic cleansing of cyclists from the township.

But it was another club, a group we had never met before. They were all on touring bikes with panniers and saddlebags and map cases and water bottles shaped like champagne magnums. They all spoke French, fluently, rapidly and with accents from Quebec. The Monday to Friday Dog just lapped up the attention as she shamelessly lay on her back, paws in the air, while they tickled her belly and blessed her in French.

We bowed to the French cyclists. One has to be polite, although for my part I would have slipped the Monday to Friday Dog a hefty kick in the ribs if I could have got closer. The Know-It-All was trying to establish cultural relations by kissing other people on the hands, but the guys didn't like it, which is quite understandable.

The Monday to Friday Dog stared at me suspiciously. She knew I had her number, and she knew that I knew she was a Separatiste in our midst. The riders from Quebec were still speaking to her in rapid French and suddenly the Monday to Friday Dog looked fully at me and closed one eye in a broad wink. A fragment from Chaucer's 'Canterbury Tales' passed through my mind:

"And Frensh she spake full faire and fetisly,
After the scole of Stratford atte Bowe,
For Frensh of Paris was to hir unknowe."

But how did the Monday to Friday Dog learn that I was born in Stratford atte Bowe?

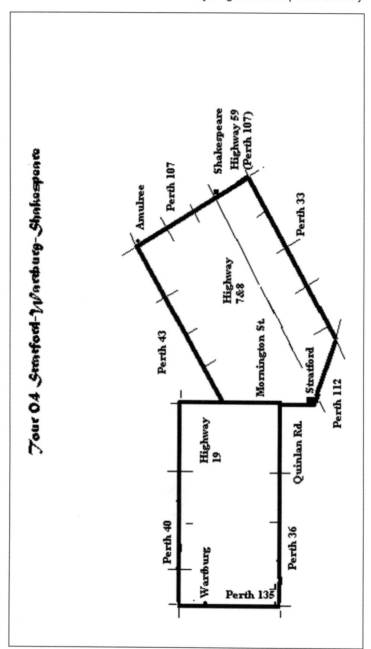

Tour 04 Stratford-Wartburg-Shakespeare

stratford - wartburg - shakespeare

Distance: 55kms.
Difficulty: novice to intermediate.
Terrain: flat to rolling to hilly.
Surface 100% tarmac.

We waddled into Tim Horton's at Waterloo and Ontario Streets in Stratford for a pre-ride coffee. The Know-It-All went on a mission to secure a table, leaving me to pay for the coffee. I flashed my seniors card (the one with the old couple disappearing into the sunset, intended to save on government funded cremations), for a discount, which did not entitle me to any further fringe benefits like the girl's phone number. It's O.K. to be seventy today, providing you're not after her phone number. I asked her where she was in 1945, but she'd never heard of it.

Yankee Doodle Dandruff and Pistachio Pete were also there and they confessed a willingness to ride with us that day. We all had our road bikes and the weather looked like road bike weather as we headed up Waterloo Street, across the Victoria Lake Bridge and joined Mornington Street.

Mornington Street turns itself into Highway 19, so we went along with it. You have to humor roads in this new, dynamic Ontario. Right at the north end of Stratford we turned left onto Perth Line 36 (Quinlan Road) and headed west. This road is quite fast and we wound it up, looking for all the world like blue and silver Tele Tubbies. (The Stratford Pacemakers uniform is royal blue and silver).

It's a good, straight wind-up on this road to the stop at Perth Road 135. In fact it's slightly over 8 kilometers for the wind-up and that's good enough to wind up the dead. At Perth Road 135 we made a right and headed north to Wartburg, where we stopped for the customary sips of Gatorade and chews at the bonk bars. Those who had no bonk bars or Gatorade simply went through the motions with slightly sad expressions.

Wartburg is quiet. In fact it's as quiet as any crossroads hamlet I've ever come across. There was nobody about and this was inconvenient because I wanted to find out if Wartburgers suffered from warts. It's possible. The Know-It-All said they might have had an infestation of toads back in the Nineteenth Century and suffered from warts ever since.

There is a signpost by St. John's Lutheran Church giving directions to Kinkora and the Botanical Gardens. I suppose those details are fine for people who carry notebooks and a superior attitude.

Pistachio Pete said he was suffering from a slow flat. We examined him minutely and then discovered the leakage was in his front tire and not in his body. The inner tube was quickly changed using Yankee Doodle as the mechanic, the Know-It-All as technical advisor and myself as recording secretary. Pistachio Pete looked on.

We continued north to the next intersection, Perth Road 44, where we turned right. The signpost at this point indicated that Rostock was straight on and Bornholm was miles and miles to the left, out Winnipeg way! I say this with all sincerity because Yankee Doodle Dandruff and Pistachio Pete are both wannabee hammerheads, and as such are both pains in the fundamental orifice. When dealing with unwanted hammerheads on a ride such as this, it is politically correct to suggest they ride a diversion for their health's sake and 'miles and miles to Bornholm' was just such a diversion. They did not, however, take up my kind offer on this occasion; Yankee Doodle had an appointment in the late afternoon and Pistachio Pete had to help his mummy. Embalming, I think.

So we rode east along this flat and little used road. The country along this road is mainly farmland and wood lots with the occasional abandoned railway. Abandoned railways always make me sad. I remember the sound of steam whistles when I was a boy. Steam was everything back then.

It's a little over eight klicks to the stop at Highway 19. Highway 19 is a busy road and there are no bike lanes. So be careful because you have to turn right and jog south for about one kilometer and then turn left and east on Perth Road 43. We waited for a couple of trucks to go by and then belted for Road 43 like the Allez-Allez boys used to when I was young and steam whistles.........!

This road goes to Amulree and it's advisable to go along with it if you want to reach Amulree in one piece. It's a quiet road passing through farms and wood lots. Not far from Amulree, and on your way, you'll see a large signboard on the right. (If you miss it then you must suffer from NHL Referee's Disease and should have your eyes checked). This tells you about the Watershed Divide and how lucky you are to be reading all about it and how you should be writing it all down in your notebook to support your superior attitude. With all this in mind you will observe 'splendid vistas' to the southeast, across the valley. The splendid vistas will also do much to support your superior attitude.

Amulree has a bevy of flashing red lights as you approach the stop sign. Don't say I didn't warn you! We turned right onto Perth Road 107 towards Shakespeare, upon which the Know-It-All adopted a bardic attitude. He did this once before when they were reaping the corn harvest. "Friends, Romans and countrymen. Lend me you ears." Fortunately, they were using a combine and couldn't hear him.

The 'splendid vistas' turned into 'gentle gradients' which is an optimistic way of saying we were into some long hills. They were granny-gear hills and there was no further conversation until we rolled into Shakespeare Conservation Area, and Yankee Doodle had to lie down on a picnic table. The people eating a late lunch at this table were quite decent about it. They ignored him until he rolled over into the potato salad. Then they moved off, muttering as they did so. Yankee Doodle said I was a rotten old man for leading him into long hills and I felt quiet proud of it.

This Conservation Area has loos in season, picnic tables, a shelter and a large pond or small lake, depending on how you look at it. The Optimists maintain it, so you should be optimistic about those gentle gradients and long hills.

Shakespeare Conservation Area is 40 klicks into your little day, but it's the best spot for lunch on this route, unless you want to eat lunch in a farmer's pasture with cows staring at you. You may also have the farmer staring at you, which could prove unnerving. No, I think the conservation area is the best place.

We continued south into Shakespeare. If you ride with the wrong crowd they will probably want to muck about in the antique stores in Shakespeare. Shakespeare has a lot of antique stores, so put your foot down with a firm hand and don't tolerate it. Antique stores come up like winter wheat. In the fall, Toronto people come down and buy a property. By the following spring, fresh antique stores have come up ready for the antique season. I once suggested a new manufacturing sector, one that manufactured antiques, should be part of Canadian industry, but the Know-It-All said I was a cynic. Pot calling the kettle black.

Shakespeare has a traffic light and we stopped because it was red. We crossed when it turned green and our Perth Road 107 turned into Highway 59 going south, and then it made the announcement that it would rename itself Perth Road 107 again. Bureaucracy is a splendid thing, ain't it? The topo map says it's Road 107 and I believe the map. Once you're south of Tavistock it's Highway 59. I think this is all part of a government conspiracy to confuse the people. It's like a Roman 'divide and conquer.'

So we offered up a prayer and rode one concession down to Line 33, turned right and headed west. It seemed the decent thing to do because it parallels Highway 7-8, which is no road for bicycles. Line 33 is fast with some bike lanes, provided you keep a weather eye open for farm traffic and commercial trucks. Mysteriously, local people call this road the Pork Road.

The Pork Road takes you back into Stratford and intersects with Downie Street/Perth Road 112. I thought I'd navigated this quite well. The two amateur hammerheads left us and I steered the Know-It-All up Downie Street, up Waterloo Street, across Ontario Street and into Tim's. I got him in the line up and told the girl that he was buying. And he did. He must have got her phone number.

I sat there drinking a free coffee and you could see that he was in pain after shelling out because he looked like he'd just drilled his own root canal. Cheapskate.

The Pedal Driven Resonating Ricochet Machine

the Ricochet machine

"If I had my time over again, I'd go to college and study ety-mology," I told the club Know-It-All, as we rode through St Marys, whooping and hollering to wake the folks. We turned onto Water Street like a stage in one of the great European tour races and headed out of town in the general direction of Wellburn.

"Is etymology something to do with butterflies and insects and other unidentified fluttering objects?" the Know-It-All wanted to know, as we puffed and panted our way up the long hill towards Highway 7.

"No. That's etymothology," I informed him, hoping that this conversation might die a painful death when we got to the next steep climb at Plover Mills.

"I think you should devote your time to the study of etymythol-ogy," he said, much later, as we started the long descent into the North Thames Valley. "You're always telling tall myths with short endings that have their origins way back in the days of the Celtic runes."

By this time we were sweeping down in a long line with Bugle Brain and Foghorn in the lead, which they do so well because they're a couple of mindless hammerheads. We roared across the river-bridge and struggled up the other side.

Anyone with a video camera would have taken some good pictures that day because we had eight riders in the group. Apart from the Know-It-All the two hammerheads, and myself there were Stuporman with Princess Amnestasia, Pearl Barley with Junkyard George, and we were all riding in the Pacemakers Club colors of blue and silver. It was a brave sight even if I nearly had a seizure as we topped the hill and rode at speed towards Bryanston.

The reason for such a good attendance on this mid-week ride was the annual pilgrimage to Ilderton. The Town of Ilderton has one of the best lunch spots in all of Ontario. The village coffee shop puts on a good meal for hungry cyclists and has the best antiqued inte-rior, including the original tin ceiling, I have ever seen.

Apart from anything else I had just drawn my pension for that month and the others were also in funds from various compensation claims. The Know-It-All is on some sort of retainer from the Ministry of Ewers and Sewers, probably a payment to stay away.

From Bryanston to Ilderton the riding becomes flatter and we soon ate up the miles, arriving in Ilderton a little ahead of noon. They sat us at a long table away from the regular patrons so we couldn't upset them. Most of us are well behaved, but Bugle Brain and Foghorn can be embarrassing when food is on the table. I remember we were riding in the City of Cambridge Century and when one of the volunteers handed out bananas, Bugle Brain and Foghorn jumped up and down and made ape-like noises. One little old lady became quite frightened and had to be revived by a St Johns person with smelling salts.

"I wish we had a watering hole like this in Stratford," Bugle Brain said, to nobody in particular. "We do," Foghorn answered. "But they won't let us in. Not since you spat all those watermelon pips on the floor and the waitress skidded into the wall with six plates of spaghetti on her arms, and the spaghetti got dumped on the customers' heads. One of the customers was bald, as I recall."

We all sat back respectfully and reminisced about the party of six wearing spaghetti on their heads with a variety of sauces - bolognese, alfredo, milanese and one other sauce with green streaks which I could not identify. We have never been allowed back there since that incident and it's such a shame because spaghetti is so important in a cyclist's diet and comes under the heading of 'carbohydrate loading'.

"Nothing ever happens in Stratford," Pearl Barley sighed. Princess Amnestasia gave a little squeak because she could never remember where Stratford was even though she'd lived there all her life. Stuporman just sat there in a trance. Junkyard George finished the last bread roll and looked around to rob another table.

"If it wasn't for Stratford," the Know-It-All said, jumping in and seizing the opportunity to spout his nonsense, "the entire entertainment world would never have had the ricochet machine." He sat back and waited for somebody to take the bait. Anxiously I tried to stop anybody leading him into a story because the waitress was trying to take our orders, standing there with her pad and pencil at a lethal angle, like a cop handing out citations for breathing too hard.

"Maybe you'd like a little more time to read the menu," our waitress said. She was so sweet and all of sixteen, so trusting and optimistic, believing that Bugle Brain and Foghorn could read anything other than beer labels.

The hook was set. The die was cast. I sat back and hoped the earth might swallow me up.

"What's a ricochet machine?" Stuporman asked, immediately dropping back into his trance. I was shocked because I'd never heard Stuporman speak before.

"Ah, I'm glad you asked," the Know-It-All said, beaming at the whole restaurant. I knew we were in for it and I frantically signaled our order to the waitress - fish and chips all round with extra chips covered with gravy; an Ontario Epicurean repast if there ever was one.

By this time Bugle Brain and Foghorn had poked carrot sticks up their nostrils. There were children in the restaurant that quickly followed their example, except one little treasure of original thought that used celery. I suppose carrot sticks had become scarce in his part of the establishment.

I had one wish at that moment, that some charitable group might seize the Know-It-All and have him carroted by jamming a large carrot down his gullet, like they did to annoying people in Spain. The Spanish are such an enlightened people. The parents quieted their children and finally our lunch arrived. Bugle Brain tried to stuff pickled cucumbers up his nose, but the vinegar caused him some discomfort and he was forced to snort them out like an elephant. Finally things settled down and the Know-It-All started his lunchtime address.

"Back in the days of silent films," the Know-It-All told us, after the traditional 'Once Upon a Time', "westerns showed gun battles between goodies and baddies with puffs of dust or rock chips flying up as bullets hit parts of the countryside if they missed the bodies taking part in the proceedings.

"But with the coming of talkies came sound effects and the art of bouncing a bullet off a rock to make a ricochet sound became a highly sought after skill. This procedure was dangerous and actors were killed and wounded when they got in the way of the bullets, which had ricocheted off rocks or covered wagons or tombstones in the inevitable boot hills.

"There was a need for a solution to this ricochet problem, and into the Wild West rode a Canadian from Stratford, ON, who invented the ricochet machine to produce these artificial ricochet effects. He was an Irishman by the name of Rick O'Shea!"

By this time Bugle Brain had a green onion in one ear and Foghorn had impressed a large mushroom cap onto his forehead which looked like a giant wart. A senior waitress came up to our table and dinged them both.

"Rick O'Shea and his All-Canadian Resonating Ricochet Machine were an immediate success. Deaths during the shoot-out scenes in Westerns dropped dramatically. Previously, it had been stunt men that had dropped, although these stand-in roles for lead actors were not highly sought after. But the Resonating Ricochet Machine solved all that. Rick O'Shea took out a U.S. and world patent for the machine which applies to this day. The original patent statement describes the ricochet machine as 'Equipment to reproduce the jumping movement, sound and resonance of a bullet ricocheting through air.' It was a fair statement because a bullet ricocheting through space makes no sound whatsoever."

We had finished the fish and chips course and were eyeing the pie menu. Bugle Brain said he would like the deep-dish apple pie, what he termed pie a-la-commode, but he was painfully dinged by the senior waitress. We gave our pie orders and the Know-It-All continued.

"The early film sets using studio backdrops gave way to the panoramic camera work of the West, which included shots of the inevitable Monument Rock. On these locations there was no electricity, so Rick O'Shea invented the Pedal Driven Resonating Ricochet Machine, which was fired up and operated by a team of retired cyclists from the Tour de France.

"As the film industry flourished, Rick O'Shea became a rich man. When the United States entered World War II, armies of pedal driven ricochet machines were used in action movies and in real battles the machines were used to add realism because the troops expected to hear these sounds when under fire. There was no end to the applications of the ricochet machine.

"Rick O'Shea had a good innings, but his era ended with the coming of the tape recorder. Overnight, Rick O'Shea and the resonating ricochet machine were out of business. It was the old, old story of replacement technology."

That seemed the end of our mid-week boredom session as we filed out from the restaurant leaving the waitressing staff in hysterics. We headed for Thorndale and the long bash home through Harrington and Harmony.

I thought we'd heard the last about the ricochet machine because the Know-It-All had been quiet for at least ten miles. It might have been the fish that upset him, but more likely the pie a-la-commode keeping him quiet and which I also found a trifle heavy.

As we rode through a deep rock cutting near Ballymote, the Know-It-All's front tire exploded like a mortar, resonating and reverberating off the canyon and echoing back and forth as it bounced from rock to rock. A eureka-type look spread across the Know-It-All's moosh. He had the look of a conquistador who had just spied the Pacific. He was oblivious of the loonie-sized hole blown in his front tire. He made echo noises and his eyes revolved, one clockwise, one counter clockwise.

"Doing," he echoed. "Doing, doing," followed by, "doing."

We leaned him against a rock and surveyed his tire. It was beyond redemption, wherever that is, because the tube was shot and shredded. He was still going, "Doing, doing," when I fished the folding spare from my bag. I always carry a folding spare, courtesy of Monsewer Michelin, on these long rides. "Doing, doing," he continued, as we inflated the spare and draped him across the saddle. We rode on.

As we got to the big stop sign in Uniondale, he awoke and suddenly made a pronouncement. "Film and television will never be the same. I have just invented the Ecological Echo Machine." He stood in the way at the stop sign until a truck driver hung on the air horn, blasting the Know-It-All with ecological echoes. It shut him up and he looked rather shell shocked as he rode with us homeward bound.

I suppose if I couldn't become an etymologist I might study ecology, or the economy or even ecumenism. My further education would become quite eclectic and away from such things as the Resonating Ricochet Machine and the Echo Equipment. The Know-It-All had been finally eclipsed.

But what of Rick O'Shea? After much archival research I found that Rick O'Shea was buried in an unmarked grave on the slopes of Snake Hill overlooking the Avon. When the gun fires to announce a performance at the Festival Theatre, the sound echoes and ricochets around Stratford. And you know who is responsible.

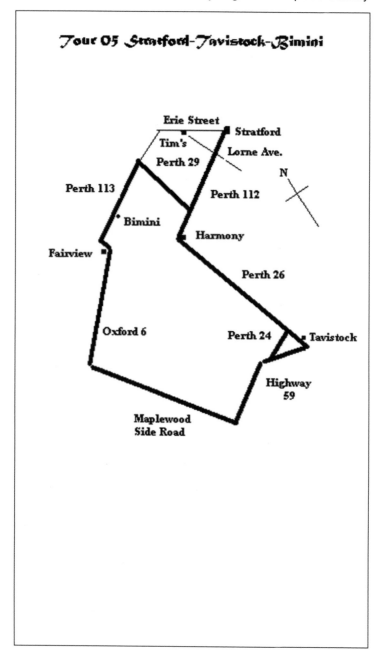

Tour 05 Stratford-Tavistock-Bimini

stratford - tavistock - Bimini

Distance: 45kms.   Difficulty: novice to intermediate.
Terrain: flat to rolling to hilly.   Surface: 100% tarmac.

It was one of those days that dawns with a cloudless sky, when the sun shines down on the righteous enough to burn your eyeballs out. The early morning was windless which generally means your outward bound ride will be against a strong zephyr straight off the Atlantic and up the St Lawrence, where it gathers strength and roars across Lake Ontario. By the time it reaches the regular morning club run of the Stratford Pacemakers, the Coast Guard are hoisting storm cones. Somehow we make it to lunch and then when we turn and head for home, expecting the wind behind us, it suddenly backs and roars right into our dentures.

Still, we had turned up to a cloudless sky, no wind, and warmth enough to grace one of the better organized deserts.

The Club Know-It-All was first to arrive, puffing and consulting his watch every two minutes. I arrived next, closely followed by Kalashnikov Kate and Stuporman, and then Junkyard George and Pearl Barley rolled in. We were glad that Bugle Brain and Foghorn, the club hammerheads, had been called away to an 'event', some type of time trial affair, which would probably give them both a heart attack.

The Know-It-All started by having a little moan about people turning up late.

"I do wish you chaps would try arriving on time," he said, glancing dramatically at his watch. "Everything backs up if we don't start off promptly at 9:00 a.m."

He should know about things backing up because he's retired from the Ministry of Ewers and Sewers, and anyway, I had never known us to leave promptly at 9:00, sometimes 9:15. More like 9:30. Sometimes 9:45, but more than likely any time with a 9 in it.

"Shaddup, you," Kalashnikov Kate told him, staring him down like the Block Commissar. "The working class only gets one day off per week, while you lead a life of total idleness."

I'd never thought the Know-It-All belonged to the class of the idle rich. As for the working class only having one day off a week, give me a break. Kate hadn't worked in ten years owing to a permanent disability caused by a severe disinclination for work.

We met at the corner of Lorne Avenue and Downie Street in Stratford. There were a few churchgoers in their cars and kids being lugged off to Sunday school. I poked my tongue out at the kids and this caused a major upset with their parents. Success!

We rode down to Harmony and Kalashinikov Kate gave me the latest geo-political line from Pravda, or Isvestia, I forget which. (Since the Mother Russias have gone in for a free-for-all market system, they could have renamed their newspaper 'Investia'). The streets were about to run red with the blue blood of aristocrats and apparently I was marked down as an aristocrat. All this was connected to my slightly high blood pressure. I wish I'd never told her about it.

"When the revolution comes, aristocrats will be hanging from the lampposts and at last we will have a worker's paradise based on the twelve hour day." I didn't know anybody who worked a twelve hour day unless he was a writer trying to make both ends meet in the middle like a bungee cord under pressure, and then suffering elastic fatigue in the process. The eight-hour day was a thing that existed when I had a job, before the world was restructured and right-sized.

This all happened while we were making a left turn at the Harmony light! With all the political stuff out of the way we rode steadily east on line 26 towards Tavistock. This is a very busy road during the week with some truck traffic, but it has some adequate bike paths to pull onto if somebody with a Sherman tank decides to pass, threatening you with a Bazooka in the process.

The road is not hilly and the country is nice farmland. Not far from Tavistock, on the left-hand side, is a curiously meandering stream. I suppose there's a scientific explanation for this stream, maybe it drained some eskers or dollmans or whatever. I said nothing in case the Know-It-All gave me a geological lecture.

We rode into Tavistock because Junkyard wanted a coffee. So we all got coffee. If you want to avoid going through Tavistock, and many do avoid it because of the traffic light, which always causes a snarl-up, you can make a right turn onto Perth Road 24. This is a slip road, which bypasses Tavistock and comes out on Highway 59 at the little bridge over the Thames River.

Whichever way you do things, you have to take Highway 59 south. I'm   sorry about that. But, be of good cheer and ride south on 59 to Oxford Road 28 (Maplewood S.R.). Turn right and ride west. This road is suddenly reborn as Road 96, and you can blame that on the trickle down and not on me.

This road is as quiet as a mouse with some farm traffic and the occasional ambulance transporting a client from Highway 59. You have plenty of scope for winding it up, playing Tour de France stuff, or you can listen to the birdies and annoy me by writing it all down in your notebook with a superior attitude.

Eventually we got to the stop sign. Straight on goes to Harrington, but we were not going there. South went to Embro, or

Timbuctoo. Somewhere like that. We turned right and rode north. There's a choice of what you call this road. Kalashnikov Kate said it was a capitalist's road, but we ignored her. It's either line 37 (of Perth) or Oxford 6. Anyway it heads in the right direction, border dispute or not.

The countryside is some of that splendid, rolling topography I rave about, and you call me a rotten old man because you say it ain't rolling, it's hilly. Whatever. It rolls right through Fairview and then you know you're back into Perth County. The road is then re-born as Perth Road 113.

The going still rolls a bit, down a really nice HILL past Camp Bimini and then up a HILL just created for the granny gear. Prudent people check their blood pressure when they get to the stop at Perth Road 26. Some kind folk had this in mind when they created a small picnic area here so that the club medical attendant can check you out. (Small picnic areas are for small picnics, so don't plan on a seven-course dinner). There are some picnic tables if you want to devour a bonk bar in a civilized fashion, or you can lie on the table pending a visit from your relatives who may come by just to collect your remains.

So much for rolling country. But you may have noticed some fine old mansions in those hills, obviously dating from the time when there were rich farmers in the land - but not now. We all know there are no rich farmers in this new, dynamic Ontario and they employ highly paid publicists to tell us that.

As the cycling club was out in strength that day, we decided to live dangerously. We crossed Perth Road 26, continuing on Perth Road 113 to the point where it runs into Highway 7/19. From here it's only a short sprint on Erie Street to Tim Horton's at the corner of Lorne Avenue. A right here (after the mandatory coffee and donut) takes you back to your start point at Downie Street.

But if you are a wimp and want the country route back home, take the first right after crossing Perth Road 26 (where the picnic tables are). This is Line 29. Ride to Perth Road 112, turn left and you arrive back at Downie and Lorne Avenue.

But if you go that way you're a wimp and you can make your own arrangements for coffee and I'll never talk to you again.

We got stale eggs. we got bad eggs

as sure as eggs is eggs

I can't imagine why I agreed to take a three-day ride up towards the Bruce Peninsular in the company of the cycling club Know-It-All. I think I must be a glutton for punishment because a day in his company is appalling. Three days of solid riding with him, listening to his prattle, his opinions, his orneriness and his obfuscation would be unbearable.

The idea was to ride up to the north of Stratford, take the back roads west through Brussels and Lucknow, then out to the Bluewater. From there we'd ride up to Kincardine and the first night's stay.

We got as far as Brussels for lunchtime. Things would have gone well in the restaurant if the Know-It-All had known how to behave. I'll admit that the waitress was as thick as two short planks. She didn't help matters when she said the meat loaf was on special and the Know-It-All said he'd like his medium-rare. Most waitresses would have just laughed to humor him and then cuffed him around the ear, hopefully with something heavy and blunt like a jackhammer. Not this one. She attempted to explain how meat loaf was meat loaf and didn't come in shades of rarity: rare, medium-rare, well done or nuked.

To say that the Know-It-All was overbearing would be an understatement. He was at his worst, and the waitress took to tears and fled to the kitchen. We had everybody's attention and I tried to hide behind the plastic flowers in the middle of the Formica tabletop. They had to call up the reserves in the shape of a waitress with a stronger mind, arms like Black Forest hams and an order book thick enough to do heavy damage to the Know-It-All's bridgework if wielded edge first.

He settled for the meat loaf as it came, simple and garnished with onions and meat gravy and fries, but he got his own way when he insisted on an outside cut. And then he asked for a side order of baked beans.

The meat loaf was burned. Well, his meat loaf was burned. He got his mouth open to complain but I kicked him on the shins with a cycling shoe and then raking him from knee to ankle with the cleats.

He left a nickel for a tip and when I found out I rode back and gave the girl a toonie. She was highly suspicious, suspecting that I wanted something immoral from her. I got out from the restaurant with my life. She really was as thick as two short planks.

We pressed on, riding on Route 20 from Belgrave, through Marnoch until we hit the Lucknow Line, not far from the Hamlet of

Mafeking.   Apparently this was the high point in the Know-It-All's day because Mafeking is named for the City of Mafeking, a siege town in the Boer War.   The Know-It-All had a great uncle in the siege, along with Lord Baden Powell, Long Tom and a mass of other goofy twerps.

He was all for pressing on to Mafeking and then continuing to the Bluewater and hightailing it up through Kintail on Highway 21. Highway 21 is a killer; a high-speed truck route with demented drivers of RVs and motor homes.   Even the Canadian Army avoids Highway 21 in case they get one of their tanks scratched.

After an hour's argument we reached a compromise: you know, one of those middle-of-the-road Canadian agreements where nobody wins. We would push on to Mafeking, it was only two concessions according to the map, and then we'd ride back to the Lucknow Line and go north through Belfast to Lucknow and then out to the Bluewater at Amberley.

I had my reasons for insisting on this route. The old Highway 86 from Lucknow to Amberley is reasonable to ride on. We had our touring bikes with panniers and barracks bags, strung with unneeded equipment which the Know-It-All said was necessary. It's just like his darned tool kit. He takes so many tools that his bike sinks into any gravel road. I'm sure he carries a drill press and center lathe squirreled away in his bike bag, just in case he needs to machine a new axle on the road.

Mafeking was a disappointment.   No great uncle, no Lord Baden Powell or Long Tom. A few goofy-looking twerps with pickups and two-fours. You know. Your average Ontario settlement!

He was quiet until we got to Lucknow and we sat in the park with a mug of Tim's Best. From Lucknow to Amberley it's a good, surfaced road. West of Amberley is the start of what I call the 'coast road', a route that takes you away from Highway 21 through cottage areas. It's the original Goderich Street and it follows the shore of Lake Huron through Kincardine, Port Elgin, Southampton and Sauble Beach, eventually saying ta-tas in Wiarton. It's also truck-free, and that's nice if you're riding a bike.

We were halfway down the mugs of Tim's Java when two young persons of the distaff persuasion joined us. They were riding mountain bikes, but there were no mountains in view so I assumed they were heading for the Rockies, just for the afternoon, you understand. They eyed us suspiciously and I offered them a swig of my coffee. They refused my kind offer so the Know-It-All tried to break the ice with his customary bonhomie.

"Whaddya want?" he said, as courteous as ever and clutching his mug of Tim's like a wino protecting his last swallow of Old Embalming Fluid.

"Where's the washroom in this here park?" the bolder of the two asked, a steely, no-nonsense, send 'em all to the moon sort of look.

"Yes, where's the washroom?" the other girl squeaked, like a mouse riding in the 'Tour de France Feminine'.

I thought the Know-It-All handled it rather well. He rose from his perch at the picnic table and pointed towards two splendidly appointed plastic Johns, the type used by construction crews, campsites and plowing matches.

"Neato," both girls squealed, one in contralto, the other in soprano, almost coloratura.

We went back to our coffee and afternoon donut feast. Within seconds both girls were back from the blue boxes. "That's gross," they both shrilled, shocked looks in their four eyes. Actually each girl had only two eyes. Two plus two equals four in the new math. I want you to be quite firm on that point. "That's disgusting," the contralto said. "Yeah, it's awful." The coloratura echoed.

The Know-It-All rose and bowed. It was his finest hour. Clearing his throat of any donut residue he gave a short, dramatic speech. "Better loo'ed ye canna be," he said, in a fake Scots accent.

I wondered if Bonnie Prince Charlie turned over in his grave at such a pun and doubly glad we were in the village of Lucknow not Paisley, where they are all amateur Scots.

The girls mounted up and rode into Lucknow high street, no doubt looking for a hairdresser where courtesy loos are there for the asking; so I understand.

"Can you believe those guys?" the contralto asked the soprano, rhetorically. "Dirty old men," the soprano replied. It was one of my proudest moments and I almost forgave the Know-It-All for being himself, but thought better of it upon reflection.

We picked up the pace on the Amberley Road and were soon on the coast road riding through Point Clark. The traffic thundered north and south on Highway 21, death-wish drivers of the worst sort all thirsty for each other's blood and we were glad we went the scenic route as we were pushed by a gentle wind off the lake into Kincardine.

Kincardine is a very Scots town so you don't make Bonnie Prince Charlie jokes. A piper was playing a lament as we rode along the lake wall, probably a lament for Charlie! We checked into a motel and the Know-It-All was overjoyed to find that there were housekeeping arrangements. On the way into K-Town we noticed a farm with a 'fresh eggs' sign nailed to the gatepost. Nothing would dissuade him from unloading our grips and riding back to 'Fresh Eggs Farm' and buying a gross or two for supper.

I was determined not to take part in this hokey bit of commerce. I thought I'd just sit back and leave enough rope in the Know-It-All's ape-like paws to garrote himself.

The farmer was mowing his lawn when we stopped by the gate. Reluctantly the man stopped the mower and sauntered over. You could see he was one of those dedicated, dyed-in-the-wool lawn mowers, the type of man not to be disturbed when he's going about his lawful occasions cutting grass.

"Help you?" the farmer asked abruptly.

"Do you have any fresh eggs?" the Know-It-All inquired, by way of an opening gambit. There's nothing like a firm move to establish your intentions, like moving the King's pawn. But you could see the farmer had played this game before. He was subtle and opened with his knight, the black piece possessed with cunning and lateral moves.

"Fresh eggs? Well, no, I don't think so. I've never heard of fresh eggs around these parts, have you, Martha?"

Martha joined us, a tiny, bird-like woman with the nose of a hawk and eyes like an owl. "Fresh eggs? Nah," she said. "Not this close to Kincardine. We got stale eggs. We got bad eggs. We got eggs with green yolks and gray whites. We got eggs like bullets and eggs with a smell that'd take tour head off. But fresh eggs? We got no call for 'em around here. You'd have to go to Toronto if you're looking for fresh eggs. You're not from Toronto, are you?"

She adopted a phony, shocked look when she mentioned Toronto, which worried the Know-It-All. "'Ere, Art. I think these fellas is from Toronna," she went on, grinding salt into the provincial wound.

Art looked as if he'd been struck by lightning because he clutched at his heart and coughed dramatically like John Wayne did when he croaked on 'The Sands of Iwo Jima'. Clearly, Art had missed his calling as a tragic actor. The Know-It-All had lost stature and dignity. He had been upstaged with no rapport to such a double-teaming.

"I don't know what the world's a-comin' to," the farmer said to his wife, turning back to his mower. "They'll be askin' for milk straight out the cow if we ain't careful."

For the sake of good order and tranquil government I knew I had to intervene. The Know-It-All was reduced to ashes and rubble. When he loses, he dribbles, and he was dribbling quite fluently down his jersey.

"Perhaps you have a few eggs just moderately stale?" I suggested to Martha, while Art shook his head slowly. "Anything will do," I continued. "Three week-old eggs would do. He won't know any difference. He scrambles eggs. It's the only thing he knows.

His brains are scrambled just like his eggs."

Martha's expression changed to that of a kindly thrush. But her eyes were still owl-like. "We got them pullets' eggs we was a-goin' ter ship ter China and say they was seagulls' eggs, Art," she said.

Art looked non-plussed, an arithmetical term of phrase often used in taverns by men calculating the score for games of bar-billiards.

"I dunno. What're we gonna do if the Chinese guvmint calls and wants ter buy our whole production?"

The time for leg-pulls was over, and the evening shadows were lengthening. Somebody had to give opportunity for an 'out' from this skit.

"Just a dozen would do," I suggested to Martha. "Just enough for supper, and then he'll be satisfied and he'll shut up."

"Ah, well, if it's just a dozen you're wantin'," Martha said and then yelled at Art. "It's just a dozen they're wantin'."

Art appeared to grumble and muttered all the way into the farmhouse and back again. He handed over an egg carton to the Know-It-All while I paid. It was cheap at the price. Not the eggs, but seeing the Know-It-All put down.

I winked at Martha and she put her hand over her mouth. We rode off, but I turned to wave back. Art and Martha were rolling around the front lawn laughing like drains.

When we got back to the motel, I sat watching television while the Know-It-All banged pots and pans together. As he broke the eggs into a bowl, I heard him mutter, "These darned eggs are fresh. They're no more than a day old." He was completely puzzled by all this, totally unaware that he'd been got at by a most unlikely alliance. He continued to mutter as he beat the eggs in the pan, finally producing a meal of scrambled fluffiness on golden toast. I suppose in retrospect he's not such a bad egg after all and like the curate's egg he's good in parts.

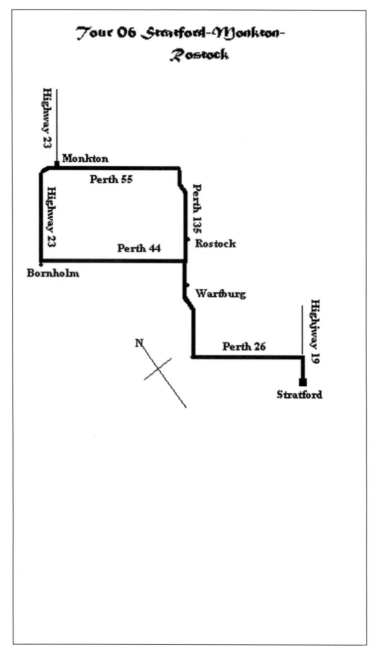

Tour 06 Stratford-Monkton-
Rostock

Highway 23

Monkton

Perth 55

Highway 23

Perth 135

Perth 44   Rostock

Bornholm

Wartburg

N

Perth 26   Highway 19

Stratford

stratford - monkton - rostock.

Distance: 75 kms.   Difficulty: intermediate to advanced.
Terrain: mostly flat to rolling.   Surface: 100% tarmac.

On the day that we rode this route, we had guest riders with us. Two members of the Roswell Aliens were camped at the Stratford Fairgrounds, Doctor Deaf and his paramour, Mucus Mem-Brain.

It is rumored that Doctor Deaf lost his license after an explosion down in Roswell, when he performed acupuncture on an inflatable doll. The Mem-Brain is pretty nice, though. You might think her aerodynamics are quite in order with very little drag or lift. But, coming from the Roswell Aliens Cycling Club, you would probably expect little else.

Four of us from the Stratford Pacemakers picked up our guests from the Fairgrounds. The Know-It-All led us, of course, with myself as navigator, Jane Eyre-Head (who promised to be a match for the Mem-Brain) and Filthy Rich. Filthy Rich is both filthy and rich and is particularly generous with coffee money during the dark days before the pension cheque arrives.

After the usual courtesies like introductions and polite criticisms of other people's bikes, we set off. The usual route pattern for anybody taking this little tour is straight north on Mornington Street (Highway 19) and then left and west on Line 36 (Quinlan Road). But as we had met our guests at the Fairgrounds we rode west on Brittania Street out to Forman Avenue, then jogged around the High School to O'Loane Avenue. Riding north on O'Loane we came to the stop on Line 36 and went west from there.

With visitors from another club, we had to show off a bit. The Know-It-All was wearing his second-best shirt, the one with the California bike motifs on it. Filthy Rich had washed that week. I'm not sure whether he was trying to impress the visitors or because he'd shown up with Jane Eyre-Head.

The Roswell Aliens, Doctor Deaf and Mucus Mem-Brain, were done up to the nines with matching shorts and shirts. And their clothes and helmets matched their bikes. The effect was absolutely awesome. I thought we might be ground into the ground, but the pace was leisurely, almost recreational. Mucus Mem-Brain was giving Jane Eyre-Head an ear bashing about how it was being an alien from Roswell, while the Know-It-All laced into Doctor Deaf about the repeal of the Old Offenders Act. You could see that Doctor deaf was very interested because his eyes revolved, one clockwise, one counterclockwise.

Pretty soon we got to the stop at Perth Road 135 and turned right, heading north through Wartburg and on to Rostock, another crossroad village.   There's a fairly large church here, Zion United Church, which is a good example of the meticulous bricklaying of one hundred years ago.

Pressing on, we rode north to Line 55 and turned left. This was the former Perth Road 9 or, as they said during the French Revolution 'La Ci-devant Route Neuf'. Well, it sounds good, but I'll bet the 'Regie de la Langue Francais' has a go at me for writing Franglais.

Just a few yards along Line 55 is a gravel road running north, Perth Road 136, going to Gravelridge. Go figure. I remember distinctly riding on this road with my eldest son, when suddenly he got a flat. Actually it was his back tire that got the flat.

That was fine. We had tools, patch kits, an anvil, lathe, drill press and a brass contraption that looked like it came off a Lee-Enfield .303. It was an adapter to fit several types of inner tube valves to any type of pump. Under the circumstances it was key to getting his back tire re-inflated, his pump being incompatible with his valve.

Of course he'd laid the brass adapter down on the ground in a nice safe place, either in the long grass or on the nice soft gravel shoulder. Safe and sound so nobody could find it. Brass adapters have qualities just like chameleons. They can change color to that of long grass or soft gravel shoulders, depending on their mood. I think it's called camouflage.

The more we looked for it the more we swore. Passing motorists stopped to listen, then hurried home to tell their neighbors. People came from Milverton to hear us curse about brass adapters in general, their heirs and successors and the missing one in particular. We cursed the history of all brass adapters, the memory of men who had invented them and finally wished bankruptcy on any company who manufactured them.

As the sun sank slowly in the west, we found the darned thing, back in the patch kit box where we'd put it in the first place. We rode home in silence, sadder and wiser for the event.

I only mention this Gravelridge Road 135 because you may have somebody you want to get rid of. Say a manufacturer or inventor of brass adapters, or any other bicycle marvel, which you are tempted to buy. I suppose you could direct him up this road with the promise that it's the back door into Milverton. Then you can ride in the opposite direction and disappear into the fleshpots of Monkton!

We rode west. Nostalgia about this event which happened years ago tuned out the constant chat between Mucus Mem-Brain and Jane Eyre-Head, to say nothing about the repeal of the Old Offenders Act coming down the pipe from the Know-It-All. I asked Filthy Rich how he was and he just grunted, so that was a comfort.

In Monkton we stopped at the Knox Presbyterian Church which is impressive, and gave the regulation number of oohs and ahs, just like tourists do.

At the stop sign in Monkton, Line 55 transforms itself into Highway 23. Actually, Highway 23 comes screaming down from the north and makes a healthy right-angled turn in the middle of Monkton, heads west out of town and then changes its mind and goes south. Roads have minds of their own these days.

Monkton has most things, but no ballet or opera house! Groceries, restaurants, Roman bath houses, chariot races. Well, not quite. We politely said hello and goodbye, staying on Highway 23, heading towards Bornholm. About halfway there's a large Catholic Church, presumably for large Catholics, called St. Brigid's. I didn't think it rated as many oohs and ahs as the Knox one in Monkton, but then I know more about bricklaying than religion.

I'm sorry I missed Bornholm. I had a bit of sand in my eye at the time, which means that Bornholm is not very big. Sarcastic old brute.

I was happy, as navigator with sand in his eye, that the Know-It-All steered us all into a left turn onto Line 44, causing a following truck driver to curse us roundly in the process.

After the sand was out of my eye, we rode east through level farmland country to the stop at Perth Road 135. I think by this time the Old Offenders Act had either been repealed or sent back to committee by the Senate. Trust the Senate not to act. They're a bunch of Old Offenders anyway.

We turned right and roared through Wartburg, frightening the little children on the way. We turned left onto Line 36 and rode like the Peloton from Hell back to Highway 19 and Stratford.

The Roswell Aliens went home to their tent and laced it shut. We were only a stone's throw from the Tim Horton's on Huron Street and they could have bought us a coffee, but what can you expect from people who claim they're aliens from Roswell? Mercifully, Filthy Rich stepped into the breach like a gentleman and we sat in Tim's for an hour at his expense.

Farm dogs are stupid anyway, and can't read a map

'everything you wanted to know about gravel roads, but were too afraid to ask.'

About five years ago, I met a couple who were riding across Canada. They had sturdy looking touring bicycles with decent treads to their tires, and enough camping equipment to choke a horse, or equip the mess hall of a bush camp.

We had a pleasant time. And I remember that they bought me an ice cream so I would talk to them while they soaked up the sunshine and local atmosphere. It was mid-afternoon and they were heading for a Provincial Park for the night. What was their best and most scenic route?

I gave them a local map and drew in my favorite roads, back roads where you only meet the occasional farm tractor, or cow herd, or plowman - 'homeward plodding his weary way' (with a six pack). A short cut between townships over an abandoned rail line. An unused road allowance fenced by choke cherry bushes and wild apples.

They looked at me very uneasily. Some measure of panic loomed in the lady's eyes. I felt it was time for an ally, so I quoted (probably misquoted) Robert Frost. 'Two roads diverged in a wood, and I - I took the one less traveled by,// And that has made all the difference.'

"Are these gravel roads?" the lady screamed, a dangerous edge to her voice and a wild and hysterical look in her eyes. "We only ride on highways, on bike paths with tar surfaces."

"But you wanted a scenic route, someplace far from the maddening crowd....." I got no further. Her swain, a likely lad of five and twenty years broke in. "Gravel roads are dangerous. You could fall off on loose gravel, and anyway there are bandits and robbers on these back roads."

The only bandits and robbers I had encountered in almost seventy summers and winters on this planet were the ones who ran for office every four to five years, claiming they were working in the public interest. If I'm ever mugged I'll feel a lot better about the occurrence.

I only weary the reader with this episode because there are many myths about riding on gravel or cinder surfaces, First of all, the bandits. Bandits who run for office do not ride bicycles and if they did, they would stick to places where they can pose in the best and most advantageous way for a photo shoot.

Second of all, the non-political bandits, the professional banditos, are all employed in government ministries where they carry out daylight robbery called taxation, and the mis-appliance thereof.

O.K. Sermon's over. Sit up straight. You may smoke, spit, scratch, swear or bite, but do it quietly. There will be a test at the end of this chapter.

In the great and glorious Province of Ontario, there are thousands and thousands of miles, leagues, knots, kilometers or spans of gravel roads, all begging to be used. They are so lonely that they come into the realm of 'lonely roads'. It follows, therefore, that these roads are far safer for cyclists than roads with fine tarmac surfaces and demented automobilists, bent on the slaughter of the two-wheeled rider.

These much derided gravel roads are there for a purpose. They form the original infrastructure of Southern Ontario (or whatever province you are riding in). The roads conform to the basic surveys carried out by our ancestors as counties and townships were laid out for settlement by the European pioneers. Each township has a survey policy and a baseline from whence the survey was run. The base line can either conform to a compass bearing, or a river or lake 'front', depending how the Founding Fathers (and Mothers) felt at the time, 150 years or so ago.

These surveys were cast in bronze, and rightly so. The lines were cut and marked, the roadways cleared and eventually gravel surfaces added. This system is called the Ontario Grid System. In my particular county, 'roads' go north south and 'lines' go east west. So, I defy you to get lost.

Having sold you on the principles of the Lonely Road, peace and tranquillity (not to mention the myth of good government), freedom from the mad automobilist, and the navigational integrity of the grid, I'll add a little more grist to the mill. Maps and guides are not only nice, they act as an insurance policy if your nerve fails and you end up on top of a ridge with nobody to talk to except a farm dog. Farm dogs are stupid anyway and can't read a map. They're about as useless as humans that can't read maps.

Maps and guides can be begged, borrowed or stolen from tourism and information offices, shops that sell maps, county engineering and roads departments, (they may not know what you're talking about) or other cyclists who have a line on local 'mappery'. If you can surf the Internet, navigating the Grid is a breeze. I use the six Recreational Trails Maps published by Advermap.

I suppose you want to know how to ride on gravel. Groan, groan. If you fall off a couple of times and sustain a nice, colorful attack of road rash on your delicate hide, you'll soon learn to stay in the saddle. Look out for loose patches of gravel, don't make sudden turns, which cause gravel to slide under your wheels. Avoid ruts and bumps. Avoid freshly oiled road surfaces. (A few years ago, local authorities sprayed gravel with a 'non-toxic' waste product intended to bind loose surfaces. It was oily, smelly, and sticky and a darned nuisance to legs, shoes, derailers, chains, tires and probably livers and kidneys. My livers and kidneys have never been the same since). I have no further advice on the matter except to say that practice makes perfect. Riding a bike is just like sex. If you fall off try, try again! (Or read the instruction manual).

Above all, use the type of bicycle that will ride comfortably on these roads. That means most modern bikes, the mountain and hybrid bikes in particular, specialized touring bikes with decently treaded tires, even the new generation of coasters, but NOT, under any circumstances, the road bike. Road bikes are thoroughbreds of the cycling world with components of delicate structure and tires as narrow as macaroni and no thicker than bubble gum. This recreational riding is not for ROADIES! (Even though I am a dedicated ROADY).

You have to be self sufficient for this type of touring or adventure cycling. If you get yourself into trouble then you have to get yourself out of trouble, or walk home. Gravel road adventure cyclists are the paratroopers of the cycling community. (When you report for duty, check your brains at the gate). But the advantages of gravel far outweigh the drawbacks, brains or no brains.

You'll need good tires with plenty of tread, inflated, but not over-inflated, to the manufacturer's standard (generally shown on the sidewall of the tire). Take a good repair kit for your bike and some extra tools if somebody else's bike breaks down. (I have rescued several damsels in distress. Dirty old man). Don't forget a patch kit and check that little tube of rubber cement. Rubber cement has an annoying habit of drying out and has a talent for predicting when you want to use it. It dries out five minutes before you get a flat and then you're left looking at a solid lump of unusable goo, not glue. So, always check. It's also a good idea if you know how to mend a flat!

You will need enough food, bonk bars, Gatorade etc for the whole day, or if you intend to join Hannibal in crossing the Alps, take enough elephant fodder as well. You must take plenty to drink; water is the best and it ain't sticky. If you take medication pills, then take 'em. If you suffer from headaches or gutsaches, take something for them. The best guide is, BE SELF-SUFFICIENT. And always take a compact First Aid Kit. Mine has a tube of gooey stuff if I graze a knee or elbow. A bandage, things that stick to me, field dressings for the occasional gunshot wound or bayonet attack. You know, simple things. And take sunblock. Then it will rain.

And now some advice about clothing. You might need a

sweater and sweat pants to go over your cycling clothes if the day turns cool. Rain gear might be useful. I prefer getting wet because it's good for my wrinkles.

This all assumes that you know about bike bags. If you don't, then go find out. I prefer the old English saddle bag, but sadly they're now obsolete. (I'm Old English and I've been obsolete for twenty years). I have a good rack with a bag, and panniers if I'm going for several days. I have a handlebar bag and proper attachment gear and a small map case strapped to the handlebar extension. It's a matter of choice and how you see your personal equipment. Obviously, if you're one of those annoying people with a camera etc, you might need to haul a trailer along.

Finally, don't fall off unless you really feel you have to. It makes such a mess on the countryside!

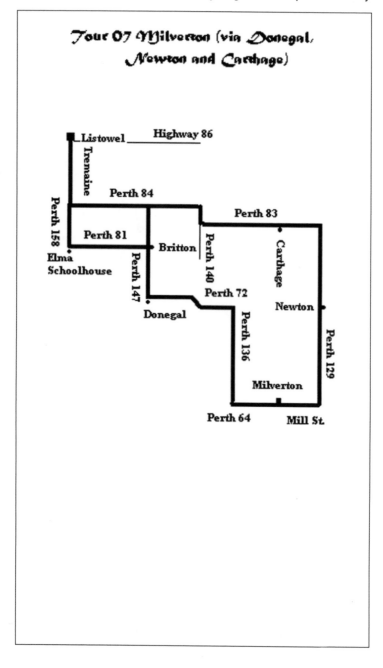

Tour 07 Milverton (via Donegal, Newton and Carthage)

Listowel - Milverton
(via Donegal, Newton & Carthage).

Distance: 55kms.   Difficulty: intermediate to advanced.
Terrain: flat - some 'gentle slopes'.   Surface: 60% gravel.

You would wonder why so many place names in the Listowel area are Irish.   Hamlets like Donegal, Newry, Gowanstown and Dublin to the south, give the countryside an Irish flavor.   And of course, Listowel has its very own St. Patrick's Festival during the week of March 17th, every year.   The wearing of the green is traditionally upheld, as is the consequent tradition of a slight churning of the digestive system and some measure of discomfort in the head.

This traditional discomfort in the head is not to be confused with a 'hammer-head'.   While the term might be construed as a painful hangover, a 'hammerhead' is an annoying creature that rides too fast and breaks with club discipline by hammering on ahead and then waiting for the club to catch up.   Perhaps, one day, we will have a hammerhead week, and they'll all be arrested and shot.

So, I was happy that two part-time Irishmen had joined us on this little tour one spring day around Paddy's Week.   Begosh and Begorrah are two gravel grovellers, Adventure Cyclists worthy of the name, and it was fitting that we ride this route together because they are both fine examples of cyclists who get off the beaten track and benefit from the isolation and tranquillity of little-used roads. (Please note a slight attempt at a 'lecture').

We met Begosh and Begorrah by the water tower in Listowel. The Know-It-All had done the driving up from Stratford and he'd moaned about the cost of gas all the way.   He's really cheap.   I remember when he took Clara, Mrs. Know-It-All, out for lunch one Thanksgiving.   Nice thought, but then he asked the waitress for separate bills!

We parked and had a look at the Listowel Rail-Trail, a section of the old rail bed that stretches diagonally across the town like a linear park and is the Listowel end of the North Perth Trailway.   It's a great pity that more former rail towns in Ontario don't follow suit and build a monument to their heritage like this, and at the same time provide a safe trail for walkers and cyclists.   Amen.

Riding through Listowel, we made our initial debut at the corner of Tremaine and Main.   It has a nice ring about it.   Tremaine becomes Perth Road 158 and we rode south out of Listowel to Line 81 and turned left at Elma School House.   This is where the gravel starts, so you'd better be a dedicated gravel groveller if you want to ride with the likes of me, Begosh and Begorrah and, at a pinch, the

Know-It-All.

This stretch of gravel goes two concessions through flat farm-land and you finally cross the abandoned rail line, the one I told you about in Listowel, (you'd better wake up because there'll be a test afterwards) at the hamlet of Britton. We turned right onto Perth Road 147 and welcomed the smooth surface because the gravel had set up vibrations in our arthritis conditions.

Perth Road 147 is a quiet road. In fact it's so peaceful that you see corpses digging their own graves in preference to staying in Listowel!

It's three concessions on this road to Donegal, and when you get there it's not a bit like the Donegal in Ireland. In fact nobody was singing about 'Dear Old Donegal' and I didn't feel 'as welcome as the flowers in May' (it was April) because a large dog of the Irish Wolfhound persuasion wandered out, sniffed me and then barked profusely.

Begosh and Begorrah both laughed like drains along the Liffey. "That dog knows an Englishman when he smells one!" darned impertinence.

Back to business. Anyone with a camera might be tempted to take a picture of Donegal United Church. Not me though. I'm a fall-en Anglican.

We turned left in Donegal and rode east on Line 72. The Irish Wolfhound eyed me suspiciously as we left and although I sang a bit of 'Mother Macree' to him, he was unconvinced.

The road has a kink, well a bend in it, towards the end of the first concession. It's at the township border between Elma and Mornington, so either they had a dispute, or the original surveyor was hung over from Paddy's Week, way back when they surveyed the lots in the 1840s.

Kink or bend, we still kept to Line 72 for another concession and then turned right, riding south on Perth Road 136. This is grav-el again and goes for three concessions to Line 64 where you turn left and east on a good surface to Milverton. The Milverton Post Office Tower can be seen on the horizon like a giant rocket as you vibrate down Road 136. Local residents claim that their tower is taller than the Post Office Tower in Calgary, but somehow I doubt that. Milvertonians are given to leg pulling.

I told Begosh and Begorrah the story about my son and his brass adapter. I won't repeat the story here because I have already dealt with the subject more than eloquently in Tour # 6, Stratford - Monkton - Rostock.

We were on Perth Road 136, heading south, when I told them about the brass adapter. Begosh and Begorrah both wanted to visit the scene, although the Know-It-All sniffed his disapproval. He was outvoted by a majority of three to one.

It wasn't far, just a bit more gravel, and we came to the scene. I was extremely gratified that the people of Mornington Township had erected a brass plaque to commemorate the occurrence. The plaque obviously memorializes many of the cuss words my son uttered on that day and which he learned in high school and college. But unfortunately I was unable to read it because the dedication is inscribed in Anglo-Saxon runes, the written language of cuss words. It will take a more scholarly person than I to translate its true meaning. No doubt after several thousands of years, a team of archaeologists will stumble upon this plaque and spend the remainder of their lives in study, trying to understand what kind of people the Anglo Saxons were.

I will say that there's an up side to all this. My son swore an oath under the blasted maple tree that he would never leave home with a brass adapter in his tool kit, unless he had a bit of red wool tied through its hole, so he might easily see it in gravel, or long grass, should he lay it down temporarily.

Back to Line 64 where we rode into Milverton. Line 64 turns itself into Mill Street and passes right by the mill. Fiendish. The main drag has a restaurant and stores, including a Post Office in case you want to mail your brass adapter back home. (Ouch). There's a parkette in the main street with a picnic table and a larger park on the east side of town with a sizeable picnic area and shelter. Loos in season, of course.

Mornington Township has its own telephone company. It's now called the Mornington Communications Co-op and was originally founded in 1919. Ontario has a number of these small phone companies and they date from the time when it was difficult to get phone service in rural areas. Very often the country doctor had the only phone. In some cases it was a doctor who started the Phone Company.

We had lunch in the restaurant although the Know-It-All complained that it meant spending money. The restaurant has a lot of old photographs on the wall, like Buffalo Bilge and Wild Bill Hiccup. They look like the Know-It-All's relatives. We held a route planning committee meeting round at his place back in the winter. He has this special 'ancestor' room with photos of his annoying forbears on the walls, right back to the ones who were all cattle thieves.

I knew he was going to muck up the day for me when I called round at his house that morning. Apparently his doctor had changed his medication without telling him. Mind you, he only takes one pill per day - for his blood pressure. But he had a little moan about that. "They used to be red and white pills," he said, working himself up into a frenzy. "But now the new ones are white and red!"

What is it with seniors and their pills?

The two amateur Irishmen, Begosh and Begorrah, were danc-ing a little jig outside the restaurant when I came out with the Know-It-All.   Several Milvertonians were watching, regarding them with suspicion as if they were both con men, which is not too far from the truth.   There seemed no rational explanation for the jig, but it was April and spring had sprung for more than a week.

We jumped onto our bikes and rode east on Mill Street through Milverton. You go past the school and down a hill, and at the bottom are Perth Road 129 and a distant tributary of the River Thames.   We turned left on Road 129 and rode north on some 'wake up' gravel. It made the Know-It-All's dentures chatter inside his head, which woke a farm dog as we passed. The dog gave one regulation bark and went back to sleep.

"Do you still have all your own teeth?" Begorrah asked him, a rather indelicate enquiry, I thought.

"I do, indeed," the Know-It-All informed him. "And I keep them in a jam jar under my bed, next to the chamber pot." There was silence after that. Even I couldn't think of a follow-up, although I became obsessed with the thought that he might drop them into the wrong receptacle in the dark of night. I found that thought quite inspirational.

Just one concession up Road 129, we came to a couple of disused railways and a real live buggy works. There were buggy parts and wheels everywhere. "I wonder if they repair bikes as well," the Know-It-All murmured, in a respectful fashion. "I guess this sort of workshop used to build penny-farthings and safeties back in the Nineteenth Century," he continued, in a hushed voice. I suppose he was right, but there was no way I'd let a buggy works adjust anything on my Schwinn. It might never fly again.

We pressed on, ever north, vibrating our arthritic joints over the gravel. The disused Listowel rail line accompanied us to our left until we pulled up at the stop in Newry. There are a couple of stores in Newry and the gas station has a lunch counter. The Community Park has picnic tables and the regulation loos when in season.

Ever north we rode, through three stops until we reached Line 83. We turned left, still on gravel and steamed into Carthage, the intersection with Highway 19.

There were no Carthaginians in sight except one small child of indeterminate gender with a dirty face. "Difficult to believe that Hannibal came from around here," I told the Know-It-All. "And he kept herds of elephants and then crossed the Alps. In those days they had Punic wars, but I never could find out who the Punics were. I assume that a Punic was an ancient warrior who wore a tunic with brass adapters instead of brass buttons."

"Don't be such an ass," he said. But his bite had gone since lunch, so I assumed his new pills, the white and red ones, were working to everybody's advantage.

We left Carthage in smoking ruins. Well, somebody was burning off the brush. Pretty soon we arrived at Perth Road 140 and took a slight jog to the north. Begosh and Begorrah thought I meant jig, but we corrected them, patiently. We then headed west again, this time on Line 84.

The gravel needed dragging on this line and my arthritis was making me rather testy. "You're rather testy," the Know-It-All said, stating the obvious.

We steamed through the stop at Perth Road 147 and rode the last two concessions back to Tremaine Avenue (Perth Road 158). Turning right on the tarmac road we wound it up back to Listowel in fine style.

Begosh and Begorrah had a crate of cold, malt Gatorade at their place and we succumbed to a few, purely for medicinal purposes. It seemed a better idea than red and white pills, or white and red pills for that matter.

But I spoke too soon. The Know-It-All moaned about the price of gas all the way back home to Stratford, until I offered to split the damage with him. He shut up after that.

That man is richest whose pleasures are the cheapest

the song of the open Road

More than a decade ago, I lived in a fairly remote corner of Ontario, a corner where settlers had taken up land and promptly broken their hearts and plows trying to farm on the edge of the Canadian Shield. Their only abundant crop was rock. They kept sheep and goats and then drifted away when the soil eroded down to the bedrock. Some went to Manitoba, others on to Saskatchewan. I hope they had better crops than the rock piles they left behind them.

Nowadays, those abandoned farms with their rocky outcrops and piles of stones are collectively called scenery. Artists paint such scenes. Poets rhapsodize about the subtle shades of light and color as the sun moves across the stony landscape. Bird watchers come with field glasses and guide books. Fishermen fish and hunters hunt. Of course, very few leave the safety of a highway or county road. That would be foolish in their eyes and full of risk. But adventure always needs a certain amount of risk.

The American essayist and philosopher, Henry David Thoreau, made some lasting impressions on my life. Two of his best-known pronouncements from his masterpiece 'Walden' are: "I never found the companion that was so companionable as solitude." And: "That man is the richest whose pleasures are the cheapest."

So, what does this all have to do with the open road, you ask? All right, all right. I'm coming to that, darn it.

To get away from the highways and the county roads and the city sheep that all go baaa together, I found solitude and rebirth along the tracks and back roads of the province. Like the swagman of Australia, I could ride those little-used by-ways on a good touring bicycle, carrying all I needed with me for a full day out of doors.

Like Thoreau's richest man, my pleasures are the cheapest, although I do believe in spending a few dollars on topographical maps. Those good old Ordinance Survey maps, with a scale of one inch to four miles (or one centimeter to two and a half kilometers if you've been attacked my metric) show all those tracks and road allowances. In some places they are quite inaccurate and then you have all the thrill of becoming lost and then finding yourself again. That's all part of the adventure.

Actually, I have never been badly lost. But years ago, when the earth was still very young, I sent a whole platoon of soldiers up the River Nile on a railway which last operated in 1902. It was a stupendous achievement because it was 1952, and they were never seen again. I assume they are still swanning around in the sunny

Sudan, waiting on some desert railway platform. This is the first time I have admitted responsibility. So remember. You heard it here.

Now, these back roads, these tracks, by-ways and road allowances. These routes are gravel, dirt, unmade, unwashed, unloved and largely unused. Already I can hear the Nervous Nellies and their captive knee-wobblers moaning. "But gravel is dangerous. I could fall off and puncture the skin on my precious little bum." Well, so what? Pick yourself up, mount up and ride on, MacDuff.

The truth is that a modern bike like the mountain bike, a bike just made for back roads, one with wide, knobby tires, is the ideal platform for the Nervous Nellies and their captive knee-wobblers to ride. There isn't a better bicycle to use on the roads and it's ideal to carry a whole day's supplies, tools and water. (A Canadian likely invented the mountain bike, and then an American pinched it and took out a patent).

I'm not saying you don't need a bit of practice to use these roads. You do. And that's because we are too dependent on the surfaced highways and expressways we need to live twelve months of the year in heated and air-conditioned automobiles.

Unmade, (or, more accurately) unsurfaced roads vary in their 'skins'. Some are very narrow and nothing more than cart tracks. These are generally closed in winter, only passable on a snowmobile. Nobody maintains this type of road, and I just love them. Then there are better roads, which are graded with surfaces of gravel. The only time I find this type of road difficult is when the gravel is freshly laid and it hasn't been rolled. I try to avoid fresh gravel and I always avoid a road if it has just been oiled or some marvelous 'non toxic chemical' has been freely sprayed onto the surface for the doubtful benefit of the user.

In the past twenty-five years, I have only experienced two cases of gravel rash upon my little pink body. Farm dogs caused both accidents, not by taking a spill due solely to the gravel surface. I'm happy to say that I have outlived both dogs.

The only other problem I experience, and it's not frequent, is the occasional auto driver of the jackass genre. His (or her) pea-sized brain gets a whole set of jollies by driving too close to me, spinning his wheels and showering me with loose gravel. If this happens to you, curse the driver in good round terms. Get the local coven of witches (they'll be in the Yellow Pages) to put a hex on him. Drive nails into his effigy, and finally, and this is desperate stuff, give his plate number to the police and swear out a complaint. None of this will do any good, but you'll feel a whole lot better. Just imagine what joy you'd get if you find this gravel-showering lout a few miles down the road and his car's broken down. Tell him you've cast a spell over him and turned his car into a permanent lemon.

But the real pleasure of riding with very little traffic far outweighs the odd inconvenience of gravel roads. I've come across riders who will only ride busy surfaced roads. They are simply missing a whole better world, which is out there for the taking. Riding the back roads, doubles no triples the opportunity for scenery and mild adventure.

So, come ride with me on the back roads. Take it easy at first and learn a slightly different technique. You may see me, a rather rotund, but dignified old man who is prone to orneryness, riding along and muttering. Avoid my companions, Bugle Brain and Foghorn. Ignore Buffalo Bilge and Wild Bill Hiccup. And above all, have nothing to do with the Know-It-All from the Pacemakers Cycling Club.

With these simple guidelines you should be in good shape to teach the song of the open road.

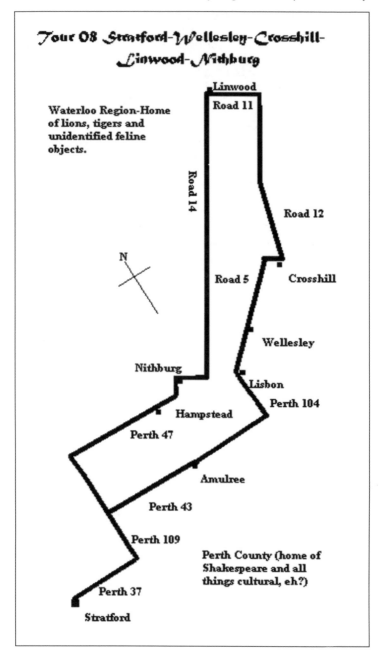

Tour 08 Stratford-Wellesley-Crosshill-Linwood-Nithburg

Linwood

Road 11

Waterloo Region-Home
of lions, tigers and
unidentified feline
objects.

Road 14

Road 12

N

Road 5   Crosshill

Wellesley

Nithburg

Lisbon

Perth 104

Hampstead

Perth 47

Amulree

Perth 43

Perth 109

Perth County (home of
Shakespeare and all
things cultural, eh?)

Perth 37

Stratford

stratford - wellesley - crosshill - linwood - nithburg.
(foreign tour).

Distance: 85 kms.   Difficulty: intermediate to advanced.
Terrain: flat to hilly.   Surface: 50% gravel.

This is an all time favorite route for me. There's plenty of rugged back road riding, but in the main you're away from traffic. Once you get near Wellesley you are firmly into horse and buggy country.

I respect the Amish and their quiet ways. I also think they're good farmers because they respect the land and don't crush it with heavy machinery. But I get ahead of myself.

The first member of the Pacemakers Cycling Club to ride this route tried it one winter and then appeared on my doorstep looking like a very tall icicle. Suspecting an Unidentified Frozen Object, I slammed the door and left the icicle standing on my porch. Within seconds the icicle had rung my doorbell again, this time hanging onto the bell push, frozen in chime! Ouch.

Upon slightly thawing out this apparition, it turned out to be the Know-It-All who had stayed in the saddle all day after walking out on Clarissa that morning in a denture locking temper when they had disagreed on some obscure point of politics. Christian charity being what it is, I took him in and poured him half a jam jar full of Old Embalming Fluid, a noble distillation capable of warming the cockles and muscles, (alive-alive-o). Droll fellow.

I have to admit that riding this 85-kilometre route in the depths of January was quite an achievement. Foolhardy too, but nevertheless an achievement. Later that evening, after the Old Embalming Fluid had sunk low in the bottle, we managed to write this little tour down in the notebook and also outline it on a topographical map.

The first time I rode it was during the following June when the Know-It-All had his young niece down from Toronto and she had brought her girl friend, who was also of young and tender years.

I knew we were both in trouble when we found out that these girls were tri-athletes, building up to an Iron Man event or whatever iron equivalent young girls compete in. I thought in terms of Iron Maidens, like the Rhine Maidens in Richard Wagner's wearisome operas, the ones who wear garbage can lids for armored brassieres. As the Know-I-All put it, "Death before dishonor," so I assumed he was going to ride with them even if it killed him. I decided to ride as soon as I saw both girls. A deep sense of grandfatherly warmth embraced me like a swig of Old Embalming Fluid, as they swung their shapely legs over the saddles and flexed their young and pliant bodies! Dirty old man.

We rode out of Stratford, north on Romeo Street, up past the Country Club to Line 37. We turned right and rode east to the end of the tarmac at Perth Road 109, turning left and north climbing a sharp hill on a gravel road. The Know-It-All went to his granny gear early that day, and I followed suit.

It turned out that both girls had names. It's extraordinary how you find these things out, but the Know-It-All had rather rudely failed with his introductions, just waving his hands in the air as if he was conducting the Beethoven Choral Symphony.

His niece turned out to be named Charlotte, but preferred to be called Charlie. Her pal was Claire, who I thought should be called Claire de Loony because she had that vacant, Toronto look about her. I'll never go to heaven. Anyway, it all worked well and we shoved on, north, up through hills of gravel.

This route has so many cemeteries that I lost count. It's sufficient so say that they all have many pioneer gravestones, so if you're into the genealogy stuff, this is the tour for a notebook and pencil.

After some good cardio-vascular stuff for me and the Know-It-All, and riding in circles and waiting for us by the two tri-athletes, we got to the stop at Line 43, turned right and headed for Amulree. Just a little west of Amulree is the watershed board, explaining that to the east is the Grand River Watershed which empties into Lake Erie, and to the west lies the Upper Thames Watershed which flows into Lake St. Clair. Clair de Looney wrote all this down in her notebook.

At Amulree we stopped at the red light. There was a herd of elephants coming down the hill, so we let them have right-of-way. Elephants gone, we crossed and continued on Line 43 to Perth Road 104 where we turned left and rode through farm country to Lisbon at Line 47.

In Lisbon you have to be canny because you're leaving Perth County and the road numbering changes. We turned right onto Wilmot Township Road 1 to Road 5. Turning left we crossed the Nith River and rode triumphantly into Wellesley.

Wellesley has a very nice park and it's easily the best spot to have lunch, even though you're only about 30 kilometers into the ride. The park has the usual amenities and there are small stores, a grocery and The Wellesley Inn for cooked meals.

In the middle of Wellesley we turned right onto Queen's Bush Road, actually the main drag, and rode to Greenwood Hill Road. At the stop we turned left and rode north up Greenwood Hill Road through delightful, hilly country. The girls were enjoying themselves, although I had already started to wilt and the Know-It-All had changed color several times.

We rode to the stop at Weimar Line, crossed, and rode further to the stop at Hessen Strasse.   You probably know that Pennsylvania Dutch is still spoken around here, although I've not heard it for many years.   We crossed and rode to the stop on Lobsinger Line, conscious all the time of how much our cardio-vasculars were improving on this ride.

We crossed to Hutchison Road, which is Road 5. Turning right and north we were in Crosshill, but we didn't follow the surfaced road, which bends sharply to the left, but rode straight north on gravel, the road still insisting it was Hutchison Road.

This stretch is quite hilly, very gravely and awfully rural. It's also a fair old ride through these hills until the gravel road suddenly bends right at an old school house and comes out on Ament Line, Road 17.

We went left from this stop and rode triumphantly into Linwood.   There is a general store and grocers shop in Linwood. The Linwood Tavern is right on the crossroad and this also doubles as a restaurant.

Turning left and south on Road 5, a well-surfaced road, we steamed down to the stop at Waterloo Road 11, William Hasting Line. This point is not far west of Crosshill - I just thought you might like to know. Crossing this road we were back on gravel, riding on Manser Road to a stop at Streicher Line. Still south on gravel we arrived at a stop on Deborah Glaister Line and crossed again, riding ever south through hills to the next stop on Perth Line 7.

Jogging to the right on Perth Line 7, we rode west to the second southbound road, turning left and steaming through Nithburg. After crossing the Nith River, we were back on gravel - and going up a hill. We all waited for the Know-It-All and then when he caught up, we took off again, which caused him some level of distress.

At Line 47 we went right and rode down to Hamstead to the stop on Perth Road 107. We continued west on Line 47 for two concessions, turning left and south on Road 109. Riding ever south we went through stops on Lines 45, 43 and 40, finally reaching Brocksden on Line 37. The notebooks came out because we were at Brocksden School Museum! Also, the Know-It-All looked like death warmed up. Continuing west it was an easy ride back to Romeo Street and Stratford.

The Know-It-All must have been quite demented because he opened up his emergency supply of beer. As for the two tri-athletes, they got themselves a game of squash with some young men from the Theatre.

The Great Bike Shop in the Sky

the cyclist's liar

I was shocked out of my reach-me-downs when the Club Know-It-All came around to see me, telling me about the death of Lou-the-Lizard, an old friend and supplier of contraband bicycle parts.

It is a sad time for those passing through our time of life. Never a month goes by and yet another geriatric wheeler passes on to the great bike shop in the sky. In memory there is the usual gathering of geezers to remember the dearly departed's life and honor his passing as a most extinguished gentleman.

We gathered around the grave while our club bugler sounded the 'Last Spoke' and a firing party exploded inner tubes to ward off evil spirits. It was late November, the end of the regular cycling season and therefore a convenient time for burials. Clara - Mrs. Know-It-All, comforted Lou-the-Lizard's wife, the Sugar Plump Fairy, (sister to the Green Bay Alpaca). But I cannot help thinking that Lou's final passing was not an altogether sad occasion for his wife, judging by her evident spirits and hilarity. In fact I would say she was rather enjoying herself in a somewhat tasteless fashion.

Lou-the-Lizard was born in Squeamish, BC. He came to Ontario during the Great Depression of the 1930s and met the Sugar Plump Fairy, his future wife, during a railway excursion down to Port Dover. In those far off days, a young man announced his intentions towards a girl by chaining his bicycle to her fence. This demonstration was an offer that Sugar Plump accepted and they were duly marinated in holy deadlock, in a double chainring ceremony.

All their married life, Lou-the-Lizard and the Sugar Plump Fairy lived in a two-bedroom house with a boxroom small enough to accommodate the occasional visiting person of challenged stature, such as a native of the former Munchkinland. They settled in Hangover, Ontario where Lou opened a bicycle repair shop. This shop specialized in rebuilding bicycles, which included the rebuild of wheels, hubs, bottom brackets, derailers, hub gears, coaster brakes, generator sets and cyclometers, the last item was the one that brought fame and misfortune to the Lizard family.

In a rare fit of zeal, Lou-the-Lizard was inspired to build a cyclometer that could be infinitely adjustable. This infinite adjustment was not aimed solely at the wheel size of the bicycle. No. Lou felt that the average cyclist needed control over the number of miles he pedaled in a day. Thus, a ride that was intended to cover 100 miles might only be an actual 80. So the Fairy (named for the Sugar Plump Fairy) Infinitely Adjustable Cyclometer was invented by Lou and patented.

This cyclometer allowed anybody riding 80 miles to adjust the recording mechanism and automatically increase the mileage pedaled by 25percent, to show a figure of 100 miles at the end of the ride. The Fairy Cyclometer could be adjusted for an increase from zero to 50 percent. Thus, the truth could be told (under grave pressure), but increased by manageable increments of lies up to a whopping great untruth of half what people actually rode.

The Cyclist's Liar was born when it was discovered that a simple adjustment to the striker mechanism could increase actual performances in excess of 200 percent of actual distances traveled.

Cycling had come of age when the sport of distance-lying took its place with other such competitive exercises as fishing and golf, both activities that operate under extreme conditions of truth variance.

Sunday club runs became mammoth rides. Distances of 300, 400 - even 500 miles were regularly achieved between church attendance and high tea at 4:00 o'clock. Even the longer stages in the Tour de France could not beat the mileages of cycling club Sunday riders using the Cyclist's Liar. The original name, the Fairy Infinitely Adjustable Cyclometer, fell into disuse, to be replaced with the more popular term 'Cyclist's Liar.' Nobody wanted any part of Lou-the-Lizard or the Sugar Plump Fairy.

As with many Canadian inventions, which were groundbreaking innovations, the Cyclist's Liar was vulnerable to patent fraud. The original patent application defined its adjustable capacity from zero to 50 percent. An American manufacturer, The Truth Fairy Company of Washington, easily dodged the patent. Their chief engineer, Joe Goebels the Third, started the distance actually pedaled with an automatic increment of 50 percent (the upper limit of Lou's original Cyclometer), rising to increments of 750 percent.

Word got to the International Olympic Committee that they were being out-hustled by the Cyclist's Liar, in particular the American variant of this gadget. Using the Cyclist's Liar was far more effective than taking performance enhancing drugs, which put hundreds of sports physicians and pharmacists out of work. And this, the IOC could not tolerate.

The crisis came when the New York Stock Exchange introduced an adaptation of the Cyclist's Liar for investors. Particularly vulnerable to this investment liar was the unit trust market, which promised out-of-sight returns for many years. But with the use of the Cyclist's Liar, widow and orphan stockholders were suddenly rich beyond belief. The crash came when Wall Street stepped in to put the widows and orphans back in their places, at the poverty level.

I was so surprised to see the Sugar Plump Fairy conducting a tailgate sale outside the cemetery. There were hundreds of bicycle parts, all contraband, including mint condition Cyclist's Liars never out of the unit boxes or shipping cartons. There was no end to the old parts that Lou-the-Lizard had squirreled away over the past century and pretty soon, the Sugar Plump Fairy was working up a land sale business. During Lou's life, the Cyclist's Liar - Canadian version - had proved a marketing flop. But with his death they became a collector's item, an icon, a must-have collectible of the baby-boomers. The Sugar Plump Fairy was cleaned out of Cyclist's Liars within minutes. No wonder she looked happy when Lou-the-Lizard finally kicked off.

I never understood why Lou-the-Lizard, like all his fellow townspeople from Squeamish, BC, suffering from a weak stomach, would settle in a place like Hangover, Ontario. I suppose the answer came when I later visited the Sugar Plump Fairy at her home. She was selling up, lock, stock and firing pin and moving to Euthanasia, Florida. There were boxes and boxes of specially formulated sports drinks based on Lou-the -Lizard's own unique recipe. I bought the lot sight unseen, or flavor untasted. Lou had created an elixir.

I am now the owner of a vast supply of powdered drink crystals rather like Gatorade, called 'Crocola'. This cure-all for cyclists is a guaranteed remedy for fading performance, Bombay Belly, underarm wetness, metal corrosion - both ferrous and non-ferrous and occasional irregularity. As a cleaner of bicycle chains and derailers it has no equal. Last November I soaked my dentures in Crocola and the teeth dissolved off the dental plates. It is effective for cleaning bright metal parts and has restored chrome work on my bicycle where no chrome previously existed.

The Sugar Plump Fairy has long gone to Florida, while Lou-the-Lizard remains in Canada, buried in a pauper's grave in Hangover, Ontario. His many friends later subscribed to a fund for his headstone, upon which is a simple inscription:

Lou-the-Lizard

Cyclist and Innovator

1919 - 2001

Inventor of the

Fairy Infinitely Adjustable Cyclometer

'The Cyclist's Liar'

In Pace Rustem

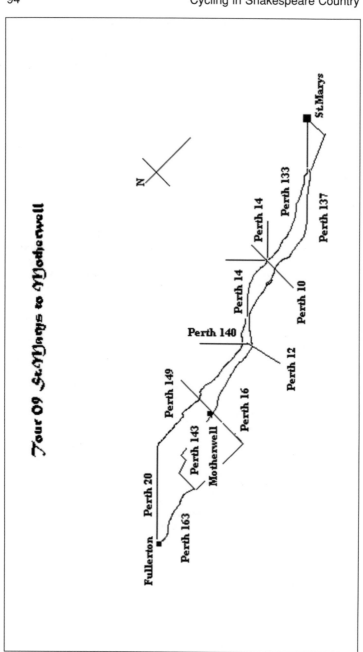

st. marys to motherwell

Distance 30 kms. Difficulty: intermediate to advanced.
Terrain: rolling to hilly. Surface: 90% gravel.

Start this scenic tour from St. Marys, my idea of a compact Ontario town. Compacted into the town is so much, including the Canadian Baseball Hall of Fame, the River Walk and the Grand Trunk Trail. St. Marys is a place to explore and to take your time doing it. If you like stone buildings, then St. Marys is the place to take your camera. From the town hall to the old post office, the opera house to the riverside stores, stone is the material of choice.

Park at the Lions Park, over near the trail pavilion. There are washrooms here and bowling greens, but they're not related. The idea is to start by crossing the Thames River by the old railway bridge which is now part of the Grand Trunk Trail. So push your bike up the slope and get onto the old right-of-way. If you want to visit the old Grand Trunk Railway station, go back onto the trail, away from the river bridge. Like many buildings in St. Marys, the old station is stone. There's a historic plaque to the Grand Trunk, and historical rail enthusiasts can drool as much as they want.

So, if you're still with me, and as I do on the frequent times that I ride this route with the Know-It-All tagging along, cross the river and ignore his prattle. The bridge is high up and the view on both sides is magnificent.

Once you're across the bridge you ride to a barrier where the official trail ends, Take Ingersoll Street and ride to Queen Street West, turn right and ride to the Beer Store. Turn right onto Thames Street and exit St. Marys. This road is now Perth Road 137 and your gravel experience starts here. A few yards along Thames Street/Perth Road 137, you may fall over the Grand Trunk right-of-way. Trail signs are now erected, so it looks as if the trail is being extended out of St. Marys.

There's no hurry. You're not Stanley searching for Livingstone in the heart of Africa. But this route does have a lot of loose surface gravel, so keep your wits about you and don't get into any intentional skids.

As you start the gravel a sign tells you that you are in Blanchard Concession 15. I suppose that gives you a warm feeling but it's never done a heck of a lot for me. There are plenty of stone houses and barns that artists and photographers would just die for and the road twists and turns like a scene from a Group of Seven painting, completely defying the grid road system of Southern Ontario.

At the bottom of a hill, another river flows into the main stream. I think it's just a tributary of the Thames, but it could be the White Nile looking for the Blue Nile, or the Upper Volga looking for the Lower Volga. You know what rivers get up to.

By this time you should have your second wind, but if you don't then you soon will. For some time now, you've been enjoying vistas, scenery galore and cardio-vascular warm-ups. Sometimes the road is high up and the river is low down. This phenomenon occurs because rivers do not flow up hills. Sarcastic old..... At Line 10 there's a bridge over the river and anybody who complains can leave us and cross to the road on the other side. And then they can go back to St. Marys and wallow in ice cream for all I care.

We will shove on, still seeking Dr. Livingstone. It was some-place around here, before Line 12, where the Know-It-All wiped out. That was back in the days when gravel was gravel. One minute he was riding along, some road technicians with shovels had strewn gravel rather thickly in places, and the next minute he'd gone. We called out to him, but there was no reply. Mind you, we didn't call very loud. You don't want to spoil a good thing and he had been a darned nuisance all day.

Suddenly he popped up from the ditch. We ignored him as if he'd dropped off the face of the earth, but he wasn't wearing it. "Pull me out of this infernal mire," he roared. Well, I think those were his words. It's a long time since and I may have paraphrased what he actually said.

We pulled him out and he certainly was mired, but not admired, shall we say. He had gone down to his waist in a pool of pig effluent and he stank to high heaven. Nobody would ride next to him and in any case his bike was completely mired as well. As luck would have it we were close to the river. There was only one thing to do and he did it. He rode right in and took a bath, bike and all, while we watched this performance from the riverbank.

Pig effluent is now highly prized by rose growers, so there's probably a price tag on it. At that time it was a just and editorial comment on his prattle.

At Line 12 there's another bridge over the river, just in case you have any deserters in the party. But press on. The scenery is worth its weight in cupro-nickel, or whatever the Royal Canadian Mint uses to make Loonies. Ride with inspiration to Line 16 and yet another bridge. This is Motherwell, all four houses of it. Nobody's put up a sign or name board telling you it's Motherwell, but I remem-ber it because I used to go bass fishing in the river. You could always get a mess of fish here because there are plenty of holes and rock overhangs. Bass love that kind of water, and they also love those little red worms you find in the compost heap.

Motherwell now consists of an antique store and a concrete sculptor.   The place is small; in fact it's so small that the Motherwellers take it in turns to be mayor. (That's the last time they allow me into Motherwell.)

But I get ahead of myself. You've been riding on Perth Road 137, which takes you as far as the village.   Turn right, cross the bridge and you're in beautiful downtown Motherwell, which I described already by getting ahead of myself.

Now! Anybody who needs exercise, you know, from the hammerhead breed, can continue up the south side of the river by not crossing the bridge and visiting beautiful downtown Motherwell and talking to the concrete sculptor.   Perth Road 143 takes these hammerheads away from you, twisting its little self and agonizing about its gravel to an intersection with Perth Road 163, a surfaced road.

The hammerheads should turn right into Fullarton where they can buy stuff like chocolate bars and lemonade and elephant forage in the village store.   In Fullarton they should turn right onto Line 20 and ride to Perth Road 149.   After a right turn they can whiz down to meet you at the intersection of Road 149 and Line 16, whooping and hollering all the way.   And it serves them right.

Just ignore their prattle and tell 'em to stop talking in the ranks.   Ride down Road 149 past splendid riverside farms.   Just south of Line 12 and its bridge, Road 149 crosses the Avon via its very own rusty iron bridge.   This is where the Avon joins the Thames and you can just feel the culture from Stratford as the two waters meet.

Mysteriously, once you're past the Avon, the route becomes Line 14.   Keep going until you get to a stop where Road 134 is at your left and Line 10 is at your right, as it crosses the third Thames River Bridge.

Choose Road 133 and continue along the river.   This takes you back to St. Marys. Yes, I know it's confusing, but just remember to stick with the river on your right.   If they've moved the river recently, then you're out of luck. Nobody said life was easy.

As you reach St. Marys, and the road becomes surfaced again, you find you are riding on Emily Street. At Water Street North bear right and return to Lions Park where you parked your car or draft elephant or bullock cart.

You are now free to wallow in ice cream and sneer at the civilians or at your friends who didn't have the moxy to ride this river route.

He was strumming on a small lute and singing

Quality time

Our most recent recruit for the Pacemaker's Cycling Club is the out-of-work actor, Anton Andante. Anton was recently injured leaping across the stage performing an arabesque and therefore unable to spend any quality time with his bicycle; those happy moments when the dedicated bicyclist cleans and oils his machine, spins its wheels and makes slight and probably unnecessary adjustments to its working parts.

"He's in pain, you know," the Club Know-It-All told me. "He took a deep bow the other day and pulled a ham string." He snickered and smiled as sickly as someone suffering from a sciatic brake cable. "He's a bit long in the tooth," the Know-It-All went on. "He's so old now he has a regular spot in the Gray Pride Parade."

I tried to ignore him and his weak humor by changing the subject. "Anton said he's been working in Wardrobe since his injury and says he's coming out of the closet next week. I wish I knew what he's talking about."

The Know-It-All changed gears as we rode up Snake Hill past the Theatre. He grabbed his hydration bottle and took a quick swig hoping some visitors from Michigan would take his photograph. Mercifully they looked the other way.

When we arrived at Anton's house, he was sitting on the front porch with his leg supported on a low stool. He was strumming on a small lute and singing his own lyrics to an Ivor Novello air:

"We'll prune the pot plant in the spring again,
And walk together with a crutch and cane,
Our knees will tremble with arthritic pain,
As we grow old and gray."

We applauded and would have given him a standing ovulation if we'd had any eggs with us to throw at him. Mrs. Andante came out to see what the fuss was all about. Annabella Andante is a faded actress, a geriactress, one who speaks frequently of her past successes on the boards and brilliance before the footlights. In her youth she had an hourglass figure, but unhappily the two components of such an assembly have now combined and meet in what can only be described as a shotglass figure. Notwithstanding, her aerodynamics are still impressive in the drag and lift departments, reminiscent of the 'Hindenburg'.

"Oh, it's you two," she said, quite unnecessarily. "I don't know if you look appealing or appalling." We had obviously interrupted her summer reading because she had a copy of Michael-Angelo's Ashes, a book of truly catholic taste, tucked under her arm.

"We only came round to adjust Anton's derailer," the Know-It-

All said, standing his ground, a hurt expression in his eyes. "Derailers have to be synchronized, otherwise you waste energy."

"Anton's wasting a lot of energy playing that lute," I said. "Ivor Novello's probably turning over in his grave and over-rotating into the bargain."

"You two have more horse fertilizer than the Aegean Stables," Arabella said. "You should have been turfed out to grass years ago."

Arabella went back into the house and I seized Anton's bicycle. In no time flat we had the derailer in parts, little springs and ratchets scattered over the pathway. We soon saw the problem. A spring had weakened which made gear shifting difficult. As we reassembled the whole thing with a new spring we were treated to some agricultural aromatherapy. There was a heck of a smell from the local fertilizer plant and we got a chest full of it back into our lungs.

I will say that Arabella is a kindly person. She brought us a tray of drinks; after all, the sun was respectably over the yardarm. A glass or two of Old Embalming Fluid in the late afternoon is just what the Cairo-Practer ordered in Ancient Egypt, and it helped endure the agricultural aromatherapy. We thanked Arabella like gentlemen.

"I'm off to the store for some ant traps. Ants are getting into the kitchen," she said, sweeping down the path through the bicycle tools like a stout Rhine Maiden.

"Make sure you buy the new, approved ant traps, Dear," Anton said, moving his bad hamstring into a more comfortable position. "The old leg-hold traps for ants are now outlawed."

"You don't know your gullet from your wallet," Arabella told him, throwing her voice to an unseen audience in the street.

We settled back with the bottle of Old Embalming Fluid between us while Anton spun his newly adjusted derailer. There is so much to be gained by spending quality time with your bicycle.

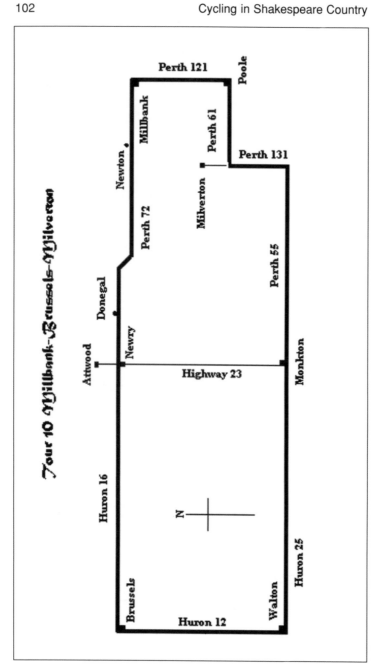

millbank - brussels - milverton.

Distance: 100 kms.   Difficulty: novice to intermediate.
Terrain: flat to rolling.   Surface: 100% surfaced.

I was having an introspective, bad hair day when I decided to ride this route, which caused me to be nasty to the Know-It-All, which in turn gave me a sense of deep satisfaction. He had to take Clara, Mrs. Know-It-All, that is, up to St. Jacobs. Consequently the loan of his car was out.

So I fired up my old pickup which frightened an elephant in the next street. Stratford was in the throes of morning breath as I headed north, the muffler bumping and sparking on the road surface. I parked in the village of Millbank and dragged my bike out.

Millbank has a conservation area with paleolithic loos and neolithic picnic tables. The River Nith flows through Millbank, which comes as a surprise to many Millbankers. There's a cheese factory, stores and Anna Mae's Home Bakery and Country Cafe.

Anna Mae's is known worldwide. I was out in Equatorial Africa years ago and I had a conversation with an Equatorial African, who asked me where I was from. When I said I was from Canada he nodded his head and when I said Toronto, he said, "Never heard of it. Is Toronto anywhere near Anna Mae's?" Which only goes to show that Anna Mae's is international.

With all this introspection in mind, I zeroed my computer and shoved off from Millbank, going west on Line 72 to Newton. Newton has two stores, a post office, gas bar, lunch counter and a park with the traditional loos and picnic tables.

Still on Line 72 I rode to Donegal where I had a short conversation with a tall dog. After a few minutes his mummy came out and ordered him into the house, giving me a filthy look in the process.

The road goes on to Newry, which is a crossroad village with Highway 23. Just north of Newry is Atwood with stores, a restaurant and cheese factory. I bought some of their Cheddar, which reminded me of Cheshire and Wensleydale.

I crossed Hiway 23 and continued west on Line 72 to the Huron County border. There's a customs post here. Well, a sign that says, 'Welcome to Huron County, Ontario's West Coast.' Some years ago I told Barnaby Grudge to bring his passport, and he did. He wouldn't have enough sense to turn up for his own wake.

The road to Brussels from this point is Huron Road 16. It's a pleasant, rolling ride and the usual rich farms, with the usual farmers trying hard not to look rich. (I heard somewhere that the President of the United States had referred to redundant farmers as, 'my fallow Americans.')

In the final approach to the town I saw that Brussels has an international airport, although bad weather had grounded all aircraft. At the intersection with Huron Road 12, I turned left to the bridge over the Maitland River, and into downtown Brussels.

This must have been a thriving and important market town during its heyday. The building facades have the strong Ontario brick construction and are quite large. For students of Victorian Ontario, the streetscape of Brussels is worth noting, although it could well do with renovation at best and a lick of paint at worst.

My computer had 40 klicks into the ride as far as Brussels, so I locked the bike to a hitching rail and went in search of lunch. There's a choice of three troughs in Brussels and I went for the one with the soup and sandwich special. I knew the Know-It-All wouldn't stick me with the check because he'd gone to St. Jacobs and probably stuck his wife, Clarissa with the check. Either that or he'd asked for separate checks, which she'd consider getting off lightly.

Road 12, south from Brussels is rolling, long shallow hills that we used to call the 'downs'. The road is good, although there is a little truck traffic. This road goes to Walton and I stopped here to make faces at some children. There is a store and a restaurant in Walton. I looked for Jim Boy, but the Waltons said he'd gone to St. Jacobs. Serves him right.

At Walton I turned left onto Road 25 and rode east to the Perth County border. The country on this stretch is flat and I had a tail wind. Pretty soon I'd worked up to a fair speed and the klicks jogged steadily by. Crossing over into Perth County, the grass took on a brighter shade of green and the road changed its identity to Perth Road 55.

There's a bit of a jiggle and joggle at Monkton where Road 55 has a fight with Highway 23 and loses. I don't know why roads do that. They show themselves up, and right by a nice truck stop too.

Monkton has another restaurant right at the crossroads or main intersection, or whatever bureaucrats say these days, but it's the sort of place where some of my family were hanged for being highwaymen. I headed directly east still on Road 55 before the OPP could get a rope strung over the hanging tree.

A shade north of Monkton - according to the map - was Monkton West. It's where the railway crossed the highway and there's a tumble down rail station there. Monkton West was so named because Monkton, New Brunswick was Monkton East. Well, I just thought you'd like to know. Now you know why some of my ancestors were hanged.

Suddenly, and without warning, I came to Perth Road 131 and the town of Milverton is just to the north. Road 131 used to be part of Highway 19 and I find all these changes to road numbers very confusing, so I don't know what it does for highwaymen. I should imagine that hanging comes as a bit of light relief.

You can go into Milverton if you like. There are stores and two restaurants and a hitching post for dromedaries, but if you've brought your elephant, the Milvertonians would prefer if he grazes out of town. Elephants leave logistical problems to clear up afterwards.

Just a little south of Milverton, and running east - west, is Line 61. This line east of Road 131 is surfaced and quiet, and rolls through farmland to Poole, another crossroads village on Road 121.

When I rode this way to Poole there were some nice hills through Mennonite country. I suspect the hills are still there. At Poole I turned left onto Road 121 and into a few more hills for the final stretch back to Millbank.

In Millbank I got myself a large ice cream and sat in the park by the river. There was an aerial battle going on, and because I was having an introspective day I imagined the crows to be Dorniers and Heinkels, and the smaller redwing blackbirds to be Spitfires and Hurricanes. Finally, the redwings drove the crows off.

"Never in the field of human conflict...." I was a boy at that time. Funnily, I have remained a boy ever since. I guess it was a most introspective day.

Aunt Thora comes back to life after each wake

popocatepetl's Revenge

I was facing a classic twenty-first century problem with my bicycle. There was a frightful clatter from the right-hand side and after extensive investigation I traced the clatter to the pedal. Once located, the noise drove me vertically bonkers and I could see that only disassembling the affected part and dosing the bearings with Elephant's Breath would give me a modicum of peace.

The real problem was not the Elephant's Breath; I use that by the gallon, having employed it for domestic maintenance on door hinges and casket lids since my father passed on the secret. In modern times it has also been used to relieve such New Age afflictions as Bombay Belly and Carpal Tunnel Syndrome, so its efficacy is proven. I hoped I would have some peace and quiet so I could spend an hour's quality time with my bicycle, just cleaning the chain, spinning the sprockets and adjusting anything that might drip oil and Elephant's Breath over my wife's kitchen floor as light relief.

So, it was reasonable to assume that the Know-It-All from our cycling club would not come round because he'd gone to a wake, thinking they were holding a garage sale. But it turned out to be a wake for one of his distant relatives, a relative who had distanced herself from him many years ago. His Old Auntie Thora Thorpe had finally popped off, or so they thought. They'd leaned the Thorpe's Corpse against the harmonium in the parlor while the family recited the usual homily about what a blameless life she'd lived, including the false accusations about the swift demise of Uncle Thorpe after she'd taken out a hefty life insurance policy on him.

All this I learned from the Know-It-All when he finally appeared while I was trying to prize the dust cap from the offending bicycle pedal using my wife's eyebrow tweezers.

"It's happened before," he said, searching the kitchen cupboard for my concealed bottle of Old Embalming Fluid. "Aunt Thora comes back to life after each wake and they put her outside in the sun until next time. After the last return from the dead, the family put its collective foot down. The next time they hold a wake for Auntie Thora Thorpe and she awakes to a new life, they're going to go into sudden death overtime and settle the old girl once and for all."

I grunted intelligently. "You should put your mouth in PARK while your brain is disengaged," I counseled him. "Right now, I'm not in the mood for wake-up reports because I can't get this darned dust cap off the pedal."

He sniffed like lawyers do on a cold day when you want some free advice. "It's simple enough. Those cheap pedals on your bike don't have screw-on dust caps. You insert a thin knife blade behind them and they pop off. Cheap pedals always clatter," he added, and sniffed again. "This whole cheap pedal technology was developed by the great Mexican bicyclist, Pop-a-clatter-pedal!" He took a belt of Old Embalming Fluid and laughed at the same time. The result was like a volcanic eruption in his epiglottis and he choked all the way back home, riding his bike over the neighbors' lawns.

I wondered if his Auntie Thora Thorpe could arrange a wake for the great Mexican boxer Puncho Villa, preserved for posterity in Old Embalming Fluid. Popocatepetl's Revenge.

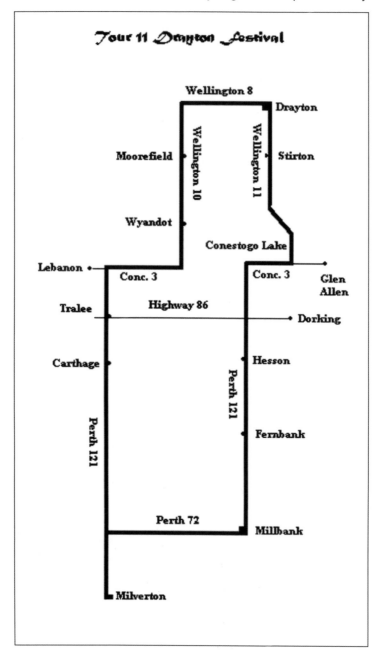

Tour 11 Drayton Festival

ᴅʀᴀʏᴛᴏɴ ꜰᴇꜱᴛɪᴠᴀʟ

Distance: 75 kms.   Difficulty: novice to intermediate.
Terrain: rolling to hilly.   Surface 100% tarmac.

We were six on the day we rode to Drayton. The Pacemakers Cycling Club sent the Know-It-All and I came along as recording secretary. Bugle Brain and Foghorn were there to represent the death-wish element, them being hammerheads, and Pearl Barley joined us as referee. Jane Eyre-Head kindly offered the use of her van and bike racks for the journey up to the start point.

We parked in Milverton, a pleasant town with all the amenities including stores and restaurants. After unloading the bikes, we headed north with the two hammerheads in the lead on Perth Road 131. You should do the same, and ride up to line 72, turn right and head east to Millbank.

As you approach Millbank there's a stop at Road 121. Turn left and ride north. The road goes up some gentle slopes through Fernbank and then flattens out through sheep farms to Hesson. Hesson is a small crossroads village, but St. Marys Church is quite a size, dating from 1892.

Continue north to Highway 86. This is a busy highway, so be careful and wait for a convenient break in the traffic. Cross Highway 86 and ride up Sideroad 15 to Concession 3. Turn right and ride east to the northbound Road 11. Your way is clearly marked with signposts. Glen Allen lies to the east and Drayton, your destination, is due north.

So follow the signs and continue north on Road 11. (Is there a slight echo in the room?) You come to Conestogo Lake Conservation Area and its main entrance to your left. On the day that we rode this route, the others all wanted a swim. I don't like swimming. I always think that if people want to swim, they should join the navy. But I was outvoted, so I had to wait for them while they all splashed about in the water, making silly noises like elephants.

I'm sure you don't want to swim, but would rather ride your bike.   Ride north and you will be on a twisty road through sharp hills. You will ride through forest plantations and have many splendid lake vistas right through Stirton and then the road flattens out and you come into Drayton, a small town nestled in the bottom of the Conestogo Valley.

You are now about 40 kilometres into the ride, just halfway. I recorded 38 klicks, Jane Eyre-Head recorded 227, and then she remembered she hadn't zeroed her computer. The two hammer-

heads recorded 40 klicks and the Know-It-All 41. Pearl Barley did-
n't have a computer, which I thought reasonable because we needed another opinion like a hole in the head.

Anyway, you can reckon on 40 klicks to Drayton. Drayton has
some stores and restaurants, enough for lunch things or emergency
supplies like coffee. There's a supermarket on your left as you
come into town. The Drayton Festival Theatre is at the bottom of
the hill on your right. You can't miss it; it's the old town hall, which
has been restored and converted to a theatre. You must go in and
see the theatre, even if you are not a Monday morning drama critic.
The only experience I had with drama was writing a skit for soldiers
called 'Lady Chatterley's Liver.' But that was a long time ago, back
when the Dead Sea was still alive!

As this is the halfway mark, lunch is conceivably called for.
There's a nice picnic area with a blue box loo just north of the
Conestogo River Bridge on Road 11, past the traffic lights.

Back in town there's a river walk at the river bridge on line 8,
just west of the traffic lights, if you like river walking. A picnic lunch
is ideal for this ride. I always bring extra sandwiches in case I get
extra hungry, which is quite usual. Those who did not pack a lunch
can go through the motions, or get a submarine in the store.

For some time now you've been riding through the County of
Wellington. You probably didn't notice because you wasted time
swimming, or laughed too much at the hammerheads riding with
you. So smarten up and start riding again.

Cross the river bridge and ride west on Line 8. There's a bit
of a climb out of the valley through rolling topography (sounds professional) until you get to Road 10, where you turn left and ride
south. The farmland is rolling with small hills and valleys, so you'll
have something physical to occupy yourselves with.

At Concession 8 you come to Moorefield which has a diner,
some small stores and a bigger food market. You might want to
stop here in case the Moorefielders wish to take your photograph.
They don't often see cyclists and never see idiots like the hammerheads.

After Concession 6 and before Concession 5, you should
come to Wyandot. It's on the map right on the edge of the forest.
However, I have to report that it ain't there. Jane Eyre-Head was
rather put out; she has a rather social conscience.

"Where is Wyandot?" she asked, as dipsy as always. "Why
do they put it on the map if it doesn't exist?"

I could see that Wyandot going AWOL would spoil her day so
I did the only thing possible. If in doubt, or when you do not have
the facts, simply make up a story and lie. Politicians do it all the time
and we vote for the brutes.

"You have to realize that Wyandot is like Brigadoon," I told her. "It only appears once in a hundred years, just for one day. And then it sleeps again and people don't see it until the next century."

There were tears in her eyes when I told her this drivel. "Oh, how romantic," she said. I felt real cheap, telling her this yarn. Pulling Jane Eyre-Head's leg is a cycling club norm, but I felt I'd gone too far with this Brigadoon tripe. But she was happy with the explanation.

By the time we got to the western reaches of Conestogo Lake she'd forgotten the whole thing. I'm rather fond of Jane Eyre-Head. I don't think she's quite as daft as she makes out and she has a capacity for making me ashamed of myself. I suppose she's just good-natured.

Keep riding south through the rest of the forest until you get to Concession 3. Turn right and ride to Sideroad 6 and turn left. Ride down to Highway 86 at Tralee. For anyone dying of thirst or hunger, Tralee is an oasis because Suzy's Restaurant is right there. I tried singing 'The Rose of Tralee' but everyone told me to shut up. Phillistines.

Ride south from Tralee and you find Smith Creek keep popping up and annoying you. Ride to the next crossroads, which is Carthage. When I passed through with my group, there was nobody about. They were probably scared of the hammerheads. We found one small boy with a grubby face who poked his tongue out at Jane Eyre-Head. I assume that poking tongues out at cyclists is Carthaginian for 'get lost.'

Considering that Road 131 used to be part of Highway 19, it's quite traffic free. We wound it up from Carthage all the way back to Milverton, and the hammerheads didn't have it all their way. Jane Eyre-Head gave them a good run for their money and I think they'd had enough when we all got back to her van.

We went into Granny's Kountry Kitchen and I bought Jane Eyre-Head an ice cream because I still felt mean about pulling her leg. She laughed and I got the impression that she only acts daft when she wants to.

Churchill's "Finest Hour" speech echoed in my ears

consTRuCTiue Roaɒ Rage

It is the socially correct stance these days to deplore acts of road rage. Never a week goes by and we hear of fresh outrages on the road. In the big cities it's all the rage, although I see no reason to deplore such acts. It should be developed as a new participation sport.

This road rage phenomenon takes on all the machismo of Wrestlemania. One participant objects to another participant's driving habits by making the appropriate gestures. Not to be outdone or out-raged, a reciprocal set of gestures is offered. There is only a slight degree of difference in attitude between rager and ragee in this new participation sport.

More and more frequently we hear of gestures and threats now backed up by challenges to a duel. Although not governed by the rules of chivalry, road rage dueling does take on the showdown customs of the western shoot-out or punch-up. Hollywood does the best job of casting horse operas under these circumstances and the contestants are evenly matched as far as physique is concerned. Only the color of hats differs; a black hat for Sir Mordred the Mildewed and a white hat for Sir Chumphead of the Chalice. It is clear whom represents good or evil attired in such costume.

It was, therefore, with great surprise that I rode into, and created, a violent scene of road rage. It was the first day I had ridden my new bike, a machine that came to me for my birthday, heavily underwritten by the whole family. I should be excused for being slightly arrogant - a new road bike does that to the best of us.

The incident happened on a lonely stretch of road where the government was laying a new surface, "Your tax dollar at work: have a nice day," sort of surface. I was having a nice day until a tractor-trailer driven by a primate in jeans and T-shirt decided to jump the flagman's orders, stick the diesel's pedal to the metal and come hurtling down the single lane towards me.

I had the right of way. There was no doubt about that and I stood my ground knowing that the law was on my side. Pragmatism has no place between tons of tractor-trailer heading towards a cyclist, whether his bike is brand new or not. My life flashed before me. Churchill's 'Finest Hour' speech echoed in my ears. I placed my hands on my hips and waited for death.

The orang-outang in the jeans and T-shirt braked and brought the rig to a halt not ten yards in front of me. Suddenly, the road gang, flagmen and spectators (supervised by the road foreman) took the side of the trucker and yelled at me. "Get off the road, yah dummy." Various other choicer pieces of Anglo-Saxon floated my way, larded with Norman French and sprinkled delicately with a condiment of Celtic. But, "Get off the road, yah dummy," was the predominant feeling.

Seeing an impasse, I mounted the bike and rode past the truck, ignoring the driver, flag jockeys and road surfacers. The rhetoric followed me; but I was bolstered up, my loins girded by Henry V's words, "Men of few words are the best men."

I rode to the nearest OPP detachment and poured my heart out to the sergeant. Like all political psychologists he promised to look into the matter, sided with me and agreed with the stand I had taken. He also promised that he would personally visit the road works and counsel all concerned. I never heard what really happened, but I suppose, like all political psychologists he sided with the trucker and the flagmen and the tar babies when he got there. My ears burned for some time after.

As a piece of constructive road rage the incident did nothing to improve community relations, but I felt a heck of a lot better for giving my opinion and pounding the ear of an OPP sergeant.

Ah, yes. The orang-outang trucker in jeans and T-shirt turned out to be a female orang-outang. And her Middle English was delicately ginger-spiced with feminist doggerel. The morning turned out to be most constructive and my finest hour for a long time.

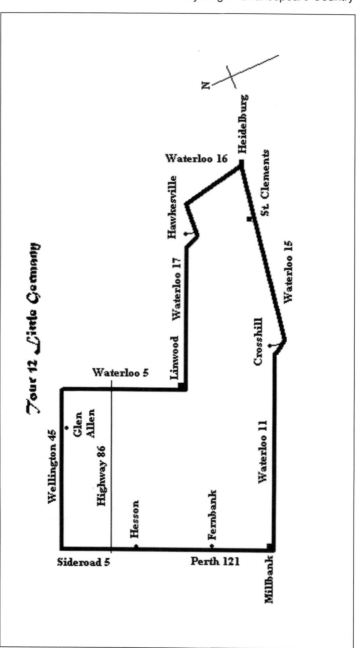

little germany

Distance: 65 kms.   Difficulty: intermediate to advanced.
Terrain: rolling to hilly.   Surface: 100% surfaced.

Our port of entry into Little Germany is the village of Millbank. We will ride through some places with German sounding names and you may wish to make some side trips to others.

One such side trip at the extreme eastern limit of this ride, which adds 10 klicks to your little day, is a visit to St. Jacobs. St. Jacobs is a step back into the past, heavily endorsed by bus tours and shutterbugs. The town of St. Jacobs is a long main street, which drops down to the river, where I can conveniently drown those riders who won't get a move on. Just a little way out of St. Jacobs is the farmers market, which is also heavily visited by tourists. I suppose if you want to bring a dry sink home on your bike or ride along with an antique bed pan banging against your rack, then the hustle and bustle of St. Jacobs will be right up your alley. There are manufacturers outlet stores and I have to say that I found my size in cycling shorts there, so you might have some success as well, looking for an air conditioned kilt! So, mount up and stop arguing. The sun is well over the yardarm and we haven't biked one solitary klick just yet. Head east out of Millbank on Perth Line 72. After about one concession you cross into Waterloo County and you are riding on Waterloo 11, which takes a fit and decides to be known as #5. At Crosshill, #5 gets fed up with you and takes a right-angled turn to the right (hmm), before plunging merrily south in its own way. You've probably stopped in the general store at Crosshill so I'll wait for you impatiently. O.K., finish the darned ice cream and turn left onto Road 15. Ride through splendid vistas, which means hills, to St. Clements. The Darling Clementines have restaurants and stores, and a community center if you wish to center on the community. Depending on which day you are riding, you will see Mennonites with their horses and buggies. Remember that they are very private people and don't want cameras shoved in their faces. I have respect for the Mennonites, not so much on religious grounds, but because they have the courage to live their chosen life style and not according to the rules laid down by the advertising maniacs and social engineers. Let's tear ourselves away from St. Clements and continue on to Heidelberg. There is a tavern/restaurant, stores and a motel if you want to drop out from this ride because you got tired riding through the hills. Me? I'm going to turn left onto Road 16 and head north to the Hawksville road, # 17. You might want to take that extra ten klicks around St. Jacobs, but I won't because my wife makes me go there to the outlet stores when I need new underwear. Oh! Darn it. Now I've let the tiger out of the bag. Retail outlet stores! Provided we manage to round everyone up again, and nobody's been taken prisoner-of-war, we'll all head west on the Hawksville road. Hawksville itself is a village only a stone's throw off the road, provided the stone isn't too large and you are an Olympic stone thrower. A signpost tells you where to turn for Hawkesville. There's a convenience store for emergency rations and a hitching rail for bikes and an itching post if you want to rub your back. I've never seen anyone in Hawkesville, so I assume they've all disappeared into Cyber Space. Continue riding west on Road 17 until you reach Linwood. This village has a tavern, two stores and multiple hitching rails - a distinction in itself. Don't tie your bikes to the hitching rails; it annoys the Linwood horses no end. In the middle of the village, the crossroads of Road 11 and Road 5, turn right and head north. Ride to Highway 86. This is Macton on the map. Most people don't know that, least of all the people who live there. There's a large church to your right, but you have to cross Highway 86 very carefully because it's busy. Now we come to the real scenic route, although it does have a few hills. Ride one concession on Road 12 and drop down the hill to the river bridge.

Cross the river (those who want to show off may swim, dragging their bikes behind them) and turn left onto Road 45, heading towards Glen Allan. Some more hilly stuff and you sweep down into the river valley again, cross by the bridge and all congratulate yourselves that you've made it to Glen Allan.

There are no stores, no taverns, no restaurants, no fast food joints in Glen Allan. But there's a nice riverside park with picnic tables and a blue box loo. Depending on your day, this park could be a nice stopping place for a snack, or lunch, or a seven-course dinner, depending what you have in your bike bag.

The climb out of Glen Allan, going west on Road 45, is truly quite brutal. So I'm so glad I sucked you in and got you tired out before saving the best hill until last. But you'll be grateful that I took you this way. It avoids suicide on Highway 86 and heads very nicely to Sideroad 15, which you soon reach, provided you did not pause for a cardiac arrest or swear about rotten old men who suddenly burst forth in Anglo Saxon, shocking the young mothers who cover their children's ears.

On your way to Sideroad 15, you will notice a right turn to Drayton. Ignore this because I've already given you a route that way and I don't want anybody getting lost.

Turn left at Sideroad 15 and this takes you south to Highway 86 which you cross very carefully. Still riding south you ride through

Hesson with its large church, through Fernbank, which is a cross-road, and finally reach Millbank again where you can collapse or jump into the Nith River if you wish.

I'm going into Anna Mae's, where I have an appointment with a rack of pork ribs with French fries and gravy, and any other forms of cholesterol I can devour.

Bugle Brain fished a bottle of suntan lotion out from his bike bag and proceeded to baste himself

Bugle Brain and Foghorn

We had ridden north-east along the ridge road one quiet Sunday morning, and just turned due east for St Marys, when we came across Bugle Brain and Foghorn as they emerged from the river trail, heading in the same direction.

I was riding with the club Know-It-All, an experience only one notch higher than riding with either Bugle Brain or Foghorn, whereas riding with all of them at the same time could cause a swift case of dementia in extremis.

"I could kill for a cup of coffee," Bugle Brain said, his voice quavering as he rode over the washboard surface of the old rail bed. "Yeah,"Foghorn endorsed. He rarely said anything else because his total vocabulary only extended to fifty words, including 'derailer', 'Gatorade' and 'bonk bar'.

It was early spring and the dandruff bushes along the track were just coming into bloom. The day was warm, but not warm enough to discard long pants and jackets; it was certainly not kilt weather. Spring weather often affects the integrity of my underwear elastic, to say nothing of bungee cord fatigue. I felt threatened in both departments and then a third element of wear thrust its ugly head into the proceedings. My chain mutinied.

I cannot really complain about bicycle chains. They have a lot to put up with and it could well have been that the chain heard mention of coffee in St Marys. We rode on, with my chain squeaking badly and frightening all the dandruff bushes on the way as they showered us with their spring blossom dust. As we rode down the main street of St Marys, I could only think that it was caused by a chain reaction.

It was fortunate that both Bugle Brain and Foghorn had coffee money with them. The Know-It-All, who is one of my bankers, was totally out of investment funds, and as a writer I was perpetually busted, after the fashion of a western bronco heading for the knacker's yard or the glue processor.

The chain squeak proved so embarrassing. Winter riding requires chain lubrication of a special nature, usually based on oil, which resists both frost and extreme moisture. Elephant's Breath has always been my winter oil of preference, having been used by two continental armies during successive retreats from Moscow in recent centuries.

Spring, summer and autumn lubrication requires more subtlety if you ride on gravel roads, those surfaces which consist of finely powdered limestone or the crushed bones of early settlers. The dust clogs up the Elephant's Breath and forms a choking mass around sprockets, inside derailers, surrounds chainwheels, and, if left to mature past April, can only be removed by the employment of a jackhammer.

So, with the arrival of the spring solstice, which I had unfortunately ignored, a different technology had to be dripped delicately onto the chain. Old Embalming Fluid is the obvious answer and I asked the Know-It-All if he had some in his tool kit.

"I used the last from the October vintage," he told me, without any regrets showing, which made him look just like the Cheshire Cat with freezer burn.

This reference to the 'October Vintage' meant that the new supply had not arrived at Junkyard's Taxidermy Supply, Funeral Director and Bicycle Repair Shop, an enterprise of remarkably strange business integration.

I was only partially quieted by the free coffee. The thought of riding home, squeaking all the way, was unbearable. In fact it was so painful that I seriously thought of walking, but only for a brief moment.

Just then, Bugle Brain fished a bottle of suntan lotion out from his bike bag and proceeded to baste himself in spite of the steady drizzle now falling to placate the local Marijuana Growers Association. He offered the bottle to Foghorn who dripped a trace element into his coffee for flavor. The Know-It-All refused graciously and when Bugle brain offered me a snort of suntan lotion I quickly exited the coffee shop and treated my bike chain against any immediate incursions of UV rays.

Bugle Brain blinked like an infomaniac who had just found a website for tarantulas, "That stuff's only for fair skin," he said. "There's no saying how it'll do on rust."

We thanked them for the coffee and headed for Stratford. We had a new product for the bicycle; one which had a narrow niche market between Whitsun and Lady Day. 'Bugle Brain's Ulterior Votive Candle Wax Chain Lube' would keep us in coffee money past the next pension increase. My bicycle proceeded silently over the Avon River and on through St Pauls.

Ridge and River Rides

One morning in April, I woke just as a weak and watery sunshine crawled up over the horizon. I thought I might waddle around to the Know-It-All's place on the next street and talk to him about my idea of including some ridge and river rides in this book, just for those who like gravel roads and road allowances and cart tracks. They are generally looked upon as demented cyclists, but I confess I have a partiality towards their policies.

At least I would be assured of a cup of weak and watery coffee at the Know-It-All's place to go along with the prospective talk about ridge and river rides. His house stands on Camomile Street, a fine example of an architectural recycling bin based on the principles of Etruscan Art. It is surrounded by dandruff bushes, an extensive area of cultivation which he refers to as the shrubbery. In fall, clouds of dandruff develop symptoms of flaking and itching in the neighborhood, causing the local people to head for Florida.

When he unbolted his front door to me, I thought the Know-It-All had a decidedly moth-eaten look, no doubt due to the spring molt, a condition not related to the dandruff bushes. When he saw me standing on his front step he promptly sent me round to the back, what he referred to as the tradesmen's entrance. He explained that Clara, Mrs. Know-It-All, didn't like people treading on her parquet flooring in the hall.

I was right about the weak and watery coffee. It was so weak that it suffered from a terminal affliction, heading for a watery grave. He stood there like a sick fry cook with one foot in the gravy, offering me a plate of Clara's rock cakes.

"Take your pick," he advised, as I took a rock cake to go with the java, and I didn't know if he meant me to make a choice of cakes or use a pickaxe on them. They were certainly rock-like and took a bit of soaking in the coffee.

We spread the maps across the kitchen table and pored over them, marking possible routes that might appeal to the demented. After much study and several interruptions from Clara, we marked up three potential routes, which we called 'Ridge and River Rides'.

These rides are not for the faint of heart, nor are they intended for extremists of the 'death wish battalion'. They are simply rides for those who want to avoid surfaced roads, who are self reliant and who like a certain amount of challenge and want to boast about it afterwards.

You need a sturdy bike for these rides with spare tubes, tools, water bottles and food. If you break down you will have to fix your bike or walk back. No rescue people will come after you and the

Camel Corps has gone to Afghanistan where they have joined our old regiment, the Duke of Athlete's Foot!

We rode all three of these rides during May, just after the Weak Coffee and Rock Cake Conference. The weather was fine, the sort of May with a warming and drying trend suitable for an Ontario spring. To make the days more pleasant, all the dandruff bushes were in full bloom, which played up the Know-It-All's allergies no end.

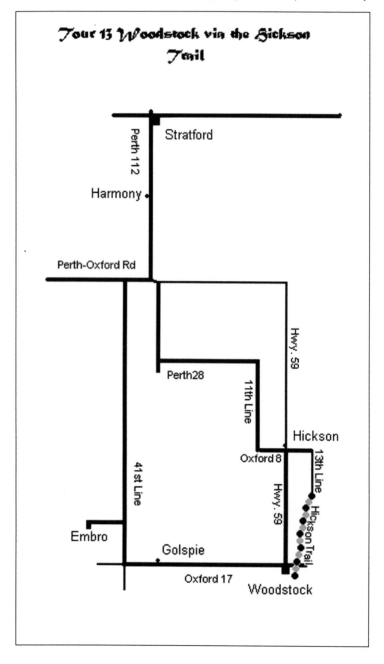

woodstock via the hickson trail.

Distance: 90 kms. Difficulty: intermediate.
Terrain: flat to rolling to hilly. Surface: 80% gravel.

It was a chilly morning in early May when the Know-It-All called at my house with his touring bike. He'd gone to a new generation of tires, which for him meant getting a deal in a sale. We were prepared for this ride with a lunch and all the other support items for an all day bike excursion.

Leaving Stratford at 9:00 a.m., we rode south on Road 112, Downie Street. This is an excellent way to exit Stratford. Some persons would say that a twenty-sixer of Old Embalming Fluid is a reliable method, but naturally I am not one of them. We had a good warm up ride through Flannigan Corners to Harmony where we stopped for a large oink-oink truck on its way to the pork and squeal plant. The only thing that gets away is the squeal. The oink-oinks disappeared into the distance and we crossed Line 26, continuing up the hill and then down the steep one to the Perth-Oxford Road.

The view from the top of the hill, before you drop down into the valley, is magnificent. That's how the Know-It-All described it and I guess he's right. At the bottom of this hill is Trout Creek, which flows east into the Thames River system. Well, that's what the Know-It-All told me and he has to be right because he's retired from the Ministry of Ewers and Sewers.

The road rises slightly and you run out of surface. Suddenly you're at gravel and the day commences. We turned left onto the Perth-Oxford and jogged to 43rd Line.

Turning south we rode one concession through spring sunshine and guys out seeing how the land was getting along, making sure the government hadn't moved their fields up to Ottawa for them during the winter. At Road 96 (which also calls itself 28, just to be ornery) we shoved on steadily into a wind strong enough to blow the dentures out of our heads. The Know-It-All, having two heads, had a worse time of this wind than I did!

We rode through Maplewood without seeing a soul. In fact we saw no human beings either and you would expect the two to be related. I told the Know-It-All about this soul to human relationship and he said not to be such an ass. He should talk. He's the sort to buy a breeding pair of mules.

At the 11th Line we turned right and headed south again. It's only two concessions to Road 88 (8) and a left turn on this surfaced road brought us to Hickson. Two Hickson dogs, a Doberman and a terrier of the rat-hunt class interrogated us. The terrier was clearly the senior dog because he interrogated the Know-It-All from the starboard beam and nearly sent him flying into the ditch. My sympathies were entirely with the interrogators.

We looked for the Hickson Trail. According to the topo map, the trail runs south from Road 8, between Highway 59 and 13th Line. Well, the map lied to us. We asked the dogs, who had escorted us through Hickson after interrogation, and they informed us that the trail actually runs south from Road 84 at the 13th Line. We thanked both dogs profusely. One has to be polite when visiting rural areas. When we looked round again they had fallen asleep outside the feed store.

With these simple navigational corrections we soon found the trail, right where the dogs said it would be. The entrance is rather indistinct. I suppose it's a semi secret. I certainly would not expect an 18-wheeler to go roaring down it, which is a comfort. But it does look a bit narrow for a railway, and as it was originally the Stratford to Port Dover Line, one assumes it was a standard gauge roadbed.

The surface is pretty good - quite a bit of grass to start with, but eventually you run on cinders. We had our touring bikes that ran well and we experienced the minimum of spills. But people with wider tires of the mountain bike might feel more comfortable. It was quiet riding through fields and woodland, almost as quiet as the time when my wife suffered from lockjaw!

Eventually, and rather reluctantly, we emerged onto Line 13, a surfaced road. The old railway bed crosses this road and heads through a sub-division in the general direction of Woodstock. As it was past noon, and we'd been three hours in the saddle, we turned left and rode to Pittock Conservation Area for lunch. We found a spot out of the wind, which chose to funnel itself down the Gordon Pittock Reservoir just to remind us of its origins in the arctic wastelands.

Lunchtime with the Know-It-All is a tedious process, most especially if he includes celery with his sandwiches. On the day we visited Woodstock, he was on a celery jag. The sound of denture-ground celery is never all that sophisticated. We were observed by a handful of ducks, who regarded the Know-It-All most gravely and without enthusiasm, and then they wandered off in search of their own peace, order and good government. Eventually he ran out of celery and started in on the carrot sticks until his dentures clogged and he had to free them off with his pocketknife. I can think of only one thing worse than a medley of celery and carrot sticks and that's crunching army ration biscuits. Sadly, we are both too old to masticate through a meal of biscuit without having our dentures re-rifled by the battalion armorer.

The sun had been in conflict with banks of clouds all morning, but eventually won the day and came through, casting its rays onto the self-righteous. This meant that our hoped-for tail wind changed its mind and backed and veered on us. As we emerged onto Highway 59 from Pittock, it blew the Know-It-All onto the gravel shoulder. I enjoy his colorful speech when this happens and he came out with a few crude epigrams I had not heard since we both served in the Arabian Field Force of 1951. It's so encouraging to observe how English usage changes so little in 50 years.

Highway 59 is not a road on which to spend a weekend. This is a busy place and trucks constantly climb the hill out of Woodstock, especially when it's open season on cyclists, generally from January to December. But we only needed a minor jog to pick up our route again. We turned right and headed a wee bit north (after he had quit his Arabian cussing) and rode at speed up to Road 74 where we hung a left and headed west towards Golspie.

This Road 74 is a pleasant, surfaced road, not heavily traveled. We enjoyed this leg of the ride; it was a change after bumping for an hour and a half over rail-trail. Golspie is not a great metropolis. I know that's sarcastic, but if you want to ride with me you can lump it. It serves you right. You shouldn't have joined.

Two concessions west of Golspie is the 41st Line. I assume it's there to this day unless some bright spark tried to sell it, just to pay down the deficit. We turned right and headed north. There are a couple of pimples - some people might say hills - and after the nausea caused by celery and carrot sticks I retched, or reached, for the granny gear. But this was only because I felt a trifle delicate in the early afternoon.

One concession north of Road 17 is Road 33. Line 41, the north-south route we followed, is only a jump east of County Road 6, a direct truck speedway running from Stratford to Highway 401 near Centreville. It's called the Embro Road because it goes through Embro, which is excuse enough.

Embro is a small town or large village, depending how you look at it. I suppose it's completely in the eye of the beholder. We, or rather the Know-It-All, decided to ride into Embro on the back road. Just north of Road 33, on your left, is Road 80, a short street, which takes you into Embro and calls itself Commissioner Street.

The purpose for our visit was to view the monument to the tug-o'-war team sent to the Chicago World's Fair in August of 1893. This team of likely lads won the world event and came back in triumph. The monument gives all the facts and I'm glad that the people of Zorra Township preserve this stone for all to see. There are five names in this team plus a captain. Their names are carved in stone, as are their considerable statistics. The largest was Robert McIntosh at 6' 2" and 215 pounds, while the baby was William

Munro at 6' 1" and 188 pounds. I guess he didn't get his full ration of wheaties. The captain's height and weight are omitted because he didn't lay onto the rope. The stone nicely describes the team as, 'Men of Might, Who Feared the Lord.'

Riding back to the 41st Line from Embro we wondered how they trained for the World Fair Tug-o'-War event. I felt they were on a diet of beef and beer; certainly not celery and carrot sticks. 1893 was well before steroids and doping of any kind, unless you think that beer brewed in Embro had some powerful qualities. There was no mention of any locally distilled Old Embalming Fluid, but the secret may be concealed in the Gaelic inscription placed there by the Caledonian Society. I don't know any Gaelic, but I suspect this inscription might be a recipe for a secret infusion used in ancient field sports. The thought of a team weighing over 1,000 pounds, all in kilts, heaving their opponents into a ditch full of muddy water, is enough to give me nightmares. No wonder they say that there's nothing worn under the kilt. What they mean is that there's nothing worn-out under the kilt!

We stayed with Line 41 and rode north. It's quite a long ride - five concessions - and then we got to the Perth-Oxford Road again. This is really a steady climb because when you get to this three-way intersection, what the Know-It-All terms a T-junction, you are at the top of the ridge again with the North Branch Creek at the bottom. We turned right and climbed another hill, one of those late afternoon hills that suddenly hit you when your blood sugar is low and you need a shot of Nelson's Blood or anything else you might keep in the bike bag.

The road drops down again and finally we turned left onto Road 112 - back in Perth County. This was the surfaced road we came down that morning. But now we had to climb the hill and by the time we reached the top at the intersection with Line 20, I was ready for something stronger than just smelling salts to bring me round.

There's only a short ride into Harmony and we did this in silence because there are a couple of pimples remaining on the road back to Stratford.

The Know-It-All went home by himself. It was a week before pension day and we both defended our last bottles of beer to the death. Knowing him he probably had something brewed from celery and carrot sticks.

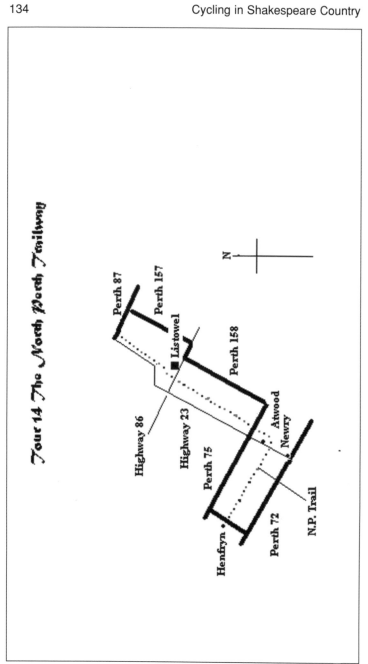

the north perth trailway

Distance: 40 Kms. Difficulty: novice to intermediate.
Terrain: flat to rolling. Surface: 80% gravel or cinder.

I was glad to hear that the Know-It-All had been forced into a shopping expedition to St. Jacobs. It seemed that Clara, Mrs. Know-It-All, needed winter boots (even though it was the month of May) and the only place to buy them in the whole of Canada was some obscure outlet at the market. Hence the absence of the Know-It-All on compassionate grounds.

It was like a breath of fresh air when I received a call from Begosh and Begorrah, the two amateur Irishmen from Listowel. Would I like to take an early season ride up in their part of the county? This proposed ride would encompass the North Perth Trailway, part of the old C.P. Line, now converted to a rail-trail.

Yes, I would. And I hastily replied in a positive way by sending the carrier pigeon back on the next northbound wind. I find the heliograph to be so unreliable at this time of the year due to infrequent sunshine!

I met Begosh and Begorrah in the village of Atwood on Highway 23, just north of County Road 72. We had a coffee in the village nosh parlor and then drove our trucks and bikes around to Henfryn, west of Atwood. Henfryn is the start of the trail and can be found with a magnifying glass on Henfryn Line, just a spit and a draw north of County Road 16 (Newry Road).

The railway upon which this rail-trail is based ran through Brussels and onwards to the Bluewater coast. But now the stretch running west from Henfryn is in private hands and patrolled by attack rabbits.

On the day that we decided to ride this route, I had just repatriated my folding bike from the mechanic in Stratford. This bike came my way for the princely sum of two dollars. (I had beaten the seller down from five, pleading perpetual poverty) in a garage sale. I then spent $100 rebuilding it with various modern gadgets and fixing the hub three speed. After that I put out about another $100 in sweat equity. The bike is over 40 years old and still ticks over like a sewing machine. I hope I can get it to tick over like a bicycle one day.

I find this folding bike useful for travel. It means I always have a bike with me in the trunk of my car, which is useful if I want to ride a new route far from home. It also annoys my wife if she wants to load shopping in the trunk and there's a bike grinning at her when she opens the trunk lid. All this I told to Begosh and Begorrah, and they laughed politely at my wit.

The idea was to ride east from Henfryn on the Trailway back to Atwood and then, keeping on the old railbed, ride north to Listowel where we would have lunch. The return journey would be decided at that time after consultation with the map and some democratic discussion.

It is three concessions of the Trailway from Henfryn to Atwood. The first concession between Henfryn Line and Road 169 has new gravel, no doubt placed there by some very publicly spirited citizens. By public-spirited I mean snowmobilers because they do so much for trail users. People moan about snowmobiles. But not this kid. It's the snowmobilers who put so much effort into preserving old railbeds.

So, I put up with the new gravel. Begosh and Begorrah were OK. They rode their mountain bikes, but I found that my folding bike wheels were a bit small at 20" X 1.75". The width was fine, but the diameter does not lend itself to a very stable ride on fresh gravel. But after the one concession of wobbling plus crossing a tributary of the Middle Maitland River, the new gravel gave way to crushed stone and cinders. In this fashion we rode on through flat arable land until we reached Atwood. There was a bit of construction going on and we had to make a slight diversion before picking up the northbound Trailway just on the east side of Atwood. Once again, the Trailway goes through flat farmland with woodlots at tasteful interludes. Our ride followed the route of Highway 23, which is just to the west of the trail. Battalions of killer trucks were heading to Listowel and it looked like Napoleon's retreat from Moscow. What happens to the trucks when they reach Listowel I have no idea because the town is fairly quiet. I have a theory that all trucks are plunged into a bottomless swamp, never to be seen again. Serves them jolly well right.

It's a little over four concessions from Atwood to Listowel on the Trailway. I think the Know-It-All's ears burned the whole way because he became the butt of Begosh and Begorrah's humor. Humor in absentia is a noble thing, especially at the Know-It-All's expense. Serves him jolly well right. By the time we steamed into Listowel, my stomach was chiming noon. Begosh and Begorrah warned me not to bring lunch because they explained that Listowel was their town and they had tickets to a fund raising pig-out. The pig-out was in aid of some obscure charity in defense of the Western Whippoorwill. I had never met a western whippoorwill because I have never been further west than Winnipeg and somehow I felt that this bird had its habitat in the Rockies, singing to the mountain goats.

We had a box lunch of fried chicken with assorted cholesterol and coffee with the mandatory donuts, which did all of my health statistics no end of good. Nobody seems to worry about these things in Listowel like we do in Stratford. Stratford people have a mean and hungry look. Well, some of them do. Maybe the fat ones are visitors from Listowel and come down in droves because we are a four-Tim town.

With a few groans we stirred our stumps and waved goodbye to our pig-out hosts. The bikes seemed rather heavy and stiff after lunch. I had noticed this problem on previous occasions when eating a cooked meal at noon and then expecting to ride another fifty klicks before six bells. I think it has something to do with hardening of the chain lubrication or sclerosis of the bearings.

We picked up the trail again, but it soon disappeared into a subdivision. It actually stops abruptly, although the map makes a green line promise that it goes as far as Line 87, just north of Listowel. Highway 23 going north from the town is busy and its main artery. Fortunately, the shoulder is wide and it was only a short ride out of Listowel to the future trail as it crosses the highway at Line 87. There are plans in the works to extend this Trailway as far as Palmerston, but of course these plans are as secret as D-Day.

So, we turned right on Line 87 and the silence was deafening. We rode to Road 157, turned right again and headed south. This brings you back to Highway 86, after you cross the Middle Maitland River. Don't worry. There's a bridge spanning the river. At Highway 86 we turned right and jogged a short way to Tremaine Avenue running to the south. On the map it is described as Road 158, but don't let that frighten you. You have a surfaced road all the way (two concessions) to Line 81 at the old Embro Separate School #2.

The country around here is what I call rich, rolling farmland. Begosh said, "What do you think of the rich, rolling farmland around Listowel?" I grunted because I had indigestion from the box lunch and Begorrah said, "Argh." In this fashion we had a pleasant ride for another two concessions as far as Line 75 where we turned right and headed west. This line converts itself into Monument Road, the northern-most reach of Atwood and makes an intersection with Highway 23. The Elma Memorial to the Great War of 1914-18 and World War II sits there as a grim reminder lest we forget. We passed by, quietly and respectfully, heading west on a good surface. The going was good and the weather fine. We reached Road 169 where the surface gives out and we were on gravel again.

We also met the Henfryn Dog, a pooch who thinks he knows all the answers and runs out into the road after cyclists and circus elephants alike. I think he is now a sadder and wiser dog because he got a boot in the ribs from Begosh, followed by a kick in the head from Begorrah. I had fallen off in the ensuing melee and was sitting on the ground amid assorted species of gravel. The dog's mummy came out and yelled like a banshee when she saw her pooch licking my face. "Put that cyclist down. You don't know where it's been." Excuse me for existing.

With this minor skirmish to our credit we proceeded to Henfryn Line, claiming victory. We turned left and rode the short distance south back to the trucks parked decently at the trail entrance.

We had ridden a good warm-up day in the spring sunshine, experienced a Listowel pig-out and emerged victorious from our battle with the Henfryn Dog. Spending a pleasant time with Begosh and Begorrah was as good as the spring sunshine, a vast improvement over the black despair I experience in the Know-It-All's company.

I thanked them for the day and drove back to Stratford. As I went past the Know-It-All's place he was outside trimming the dandruff bushes under Clara's watchful eye. I ignored him, but I knew he'd spotted my bike in back of the pickup and I knew he'd be round as soon as Clara turned her back. Hastily, I hid my fresh bottle of Old Embalming Fluid in the eavestrough.

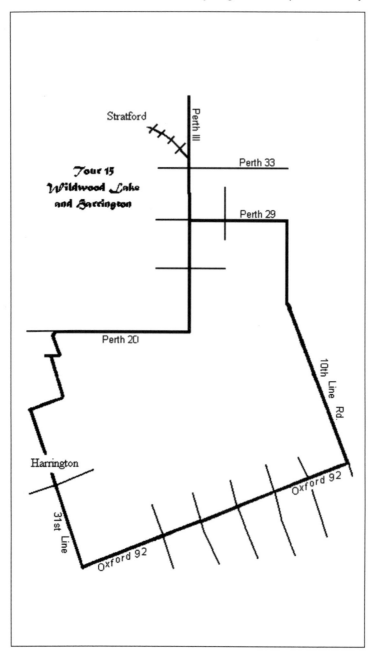

ɯilɔɯooɔ lake aɳɔ haʀʀiɳgtoɳ

Distance: 50kms. Difficulty: Intermediate.
Terrain: rolling to hilly. Surface: 80% gravel.

I think I told you that the Know-It-All is retired and drawing his pension from the Ministry of Ewers and Sewers. Well, we were riding around Stratford recently and he insisted on calling in at the water treatment plant, a sewage works by any other name. He said that raw sewage goes through one end of the Super Sanitary Sewage System and comes out the other end as bottled spring water. He properly put me off and I refused to ride with him and also made a mental note to give up the bottled spring water.

It was springtime in the Rockies and therefore springtime in Eastern Canada where we live, both sides of the country being in the same hemisphere. And as it was spring, a young man's fancy etc... In this case it was Filthy Rich, who is filthy and rich and not altogether young. Still, you can't have everything, as the guy said when his mother-in-law drove his new car off a precipice. Filthy Rich had finally found himself a girlfriend, a mournful-looking woman, called Ava Cadaver.

Ava Cadaver gave me the shivers because she was a bag of bones on wheels. She wore cycling clothes all in black and rode a black mountain bike. They arrived at my place after I had quit on the Know-It-All and refused to ride with him. Filthy Rich wanted me to take them both on a scenic jaunt, not too long, but something to give them a good workout. I noticed he'd taken a bath since meeting Ava Cadaver and he smelled like the sweet smell of success as a result. I had no idea what his bath water might do to the Super Sanitary Sewage System, but I had absolutely no intention of calling the Know-It-All to find out.

Ava Cadaver had one of those funeral parlor voices, a sort of quavery contralto you generally hear at the back of the church and put down to your own Auntie Ethel who's working at getting a place in heaven. Mind you Ava Cadaver didn't sing and I think the world is a better place because of that. She simply whined and complained until I almost felt like I'd rather ride with the Know-It-All again. Not completely, though.

So, like a good guide I told them about a gravel road ride down to the upper reaches of Wildwood Lake and Harrington and back over the ridge. It was a reasonable day, not too cold with the normal wind for May, which means blowing from every point of the compass, but not all at once. We started off and I took them out of Stratford via Romeo Street South on the old railbed by the mill. It's only one concession and we emerged onto Road 111 at County Road 33. Ava Cadaver had a little moan about the gravel and Filthy Rich looked like he was regretting enlistment when boarding a troop ship. Serves him right.

We rode south on Road 111, crossing Line 29 and County Road 26, finally stopping for a drink of water and a general moan session at Line 20. Filthy Rich offered to lower Ava Cadaver's saddle to make her more comfortable. But I knew that wouldn't work, and I was right. She was just a chronic moaner.

I made them turn right onto Line 20 and Ava Cadaver perked up a bit because there was a cemetery quite close and I thought she might want to meet all the other cadavers. This is splendid ridge country around here with little streams, and farms with cows and sheep and giraffes when in season. Ava Cadaver would have none of it and I started to feel sorry for Filthy Rich if he intended putting up with her for the rest of his days.

We shoved on and crossed Road 112 and then County Road 113. This road is surfaced, but it has a hill, which produced moans of a mega mien. Filthy Rich is generally quite sunny of disposition and generous to a fault if other cyclists are short of the makins when it comes to coffee time.

But Dame Fortune smiled on us as we muscled it up the hill. Pogey and Bess caught up with us riding their tandem bicycle. They have adapted this into an all-terrain bike and it's a very useful machine provided that the two riders are completely in cync with each other. I could not imagine in my wildest dreams that Filthy Rich and Ava Cadaver could ride such a machine without a great deal of domestic disturbance.

Pogey and Bess are no trouble and they offered to ride with us, which pleased me immensely because I thought they might get Ava Cadaver to lighten up. I was right, and I frequently am right, although the world never sees it that way. Pogey and Filthy Rich get along just fine - they always have - and Bess has a capacity for hearing complaints, and pretty soon Ava Cadaver was pouring out her heart, bypass and all.

The day settled down to a dull roar and when we reached the schoolhouse we hung a left onto Road 114 and rode south over gravel. This road has an alarming kink - I think it's what a surveyor calls a 'correction'. Kink or no kink, we rode on and were joined by Line 9 from our right, which seemed perfectly civil of it. At the Perth-Oxford Road, we stopped, only to hear Ava Cadaver yakking about her rheumatism to Bess. Bess looked like she'd just emerged from an artillery barrage, all shell-shocked. So we ignored Ava Cadaver and turned right. We went past 33rd Line and turned left onto 31st Line.

After some technical gravel riding, where I fell off and cursed at nobody in particular, we crossed the Trout Creek end of Wildwood Lake. The bridge here is one of those featureless concrete structures designed to complement the Early American Odeon mentality. Just past the bridge is a waterfowl viewing area, which is fine for those who are into such things, but I tend to categorize bird watching with the art of observing paint dry.

We came out onto County Road 28, just west of Harrington, at the old schoolhouse that now serves as a community center. There is a steep gravel hill, but I am powerless to change it. It's been there since time immemorial and you'll just have to lump it. We rode up this hill as best we could, pausing at the top for some water and a chew at the bonk bars. Filthy Rich gave Ava Cadaver a chewy, glutinous bonk bar and it stuck both of her dental plates together and silenced her.

We soon came to another surfaced road, County Road 25 and we turned left, riding east for three concessions as far as the intersection with County Road 6, the Embro Road. Crossing the Embro Road we pushed on for five concessions of gravel and ridge riding, until we reached the 10th Line.

The glutinous bonk bar was a fine thing and kept Ada Cadaver quiet. It was as good as a scold's bride, a contraption made from iron and used to silence talkative women. It's probably quite politically incorrect these days, but I can't help thinking that our ancestors must have been enlightened men when you think of such aids to peace and tranquility like the iron scold's bride and the ducking stool and the pillory.

But enlightenment apart, some black clouds were gathering above the ridge and I thought it prudent to run for home. There was a sudden chill in the air as we turned left onto 10th Line, heading north towards Stratford. The black cloud brought a bit of wind at our backs and we wound it up all the way over gravel, crossing County Road 28, the Maplewood Road, Perth-Oxford Road and County Road 26, the Tavistock Road. Once you cross the Perth-Oxford border, 10th Line changes to Road 109. Don't worry, it's just bureaucracy.

By the time we got to Line 29 it started to rain, those raindrops designed to bring out the flowers. The rain partially diluted the glutinous bonk bar and Ava Cadaver started moaning again. But by now I was case hardened to her moans and just detailed Bess to ride at Ava's side, which was difficult when you consider she was stoker on the tandem!

We turned left onto Line 29 and flogged it all the way over three concessions back to Flannigan Corners on Road 112. From there it was only a short wind-up into Stratford. There's a coffee

shop at Lorne Avenue where Filthy Rich took us for various
comestibles. He bought Ava Cadaver a large, sticky bun plastered
with frosting and cinnamon, which was about the size of a land
mine. That really jammed her dentures together. I haven't seen
Ada Cadaver since then. Filthy Rich seems quite happy and I
sense that he's dropped her.

And feeds him by shoving
a mess tin of beans under the door every four hours

epílogue

as the sun sinks slowly in the wet

Alas, we come to the end of this chapter is the life of the Stratford Pacemakers Cycling Club. Not that this is the last chapter. There will be others, stories to be told as long as the Little Fat Guy has breath in his body and coffee money in his pocket.

But just now, Hydro has pulled the plug on the word processor. Just a temporary condition until the bill's paid, they say. The Little Fat Guy will light a candle to read by and he'll put all the club characters back into the toy box, the Know-It-All first, placed on his bed of nails, face down, although a stake through the heart might be more appropriate.

Buffalo Bilge and Wild Bill Hiccup with Bottom Line Bertie and Spread Sheet Stanley go next. The Great Oink has a corner of his own, just in case he rolls over during the long nuclear night, crushing somebody. Junkyard George complains constantly about how much junk he'll miss during the winter. Kalashnikov Kate still breathes the fire and brimstone of social revolution as she goes into the box, followed by Jane Eyre-Head as bewildered as ever. Stuporman gazes into space and says nothing, but occasionally grunts while Pearl Barley mumbles incessantly.

We must never forget Clarissa, Mrs. Know-It-All, that is. No woman should suffer like that, but as she rightly says, love at her age is just a process of carbon dating.

Princess Amnestasia and Yankee Doodle Dandruff are an item - big time, and they go into the toy box side by each. How else? Holding hands they sleep through the cyber night.

Filthy Rich is still filthy and rich and nobody wants him in the toy box, but that's too bad, they'll have to lump it. We have to make room for Pogey and Bess, the well-known social activists, leaving a special corner for Bugle Brain and Foghorn.

The lid is ready for the toy box now. Nobody's forgotten. They're all battened down and ready for another winter's hibernation. But wait. We have to remember the most important character of them all, the Keeper of the Toy Box. We forgot the Little Fat Guy's wife, who sharpens his pencils and feeds him by shoving a mess tin of beans under the door every four hours. The Little Fat Guy's wife, the Celestial Editor and Keeper of the Toy Box, is the only character with any sense out of the whole lot.

But fear not. Like MacArthur, we shall return.